"If you cannot sing like angels
If you cannot preach like Paul . . ."

William L. Dawson,
"There is a Balm in Gilead"

~

If you cannot preach like Paul
then do what Paul did;
don't just say what Paul said.

If You Cannot Preach Like Paul . . .

NANCY LAMMERS GROSS

William B. Eerdmans Publishing Company

Grand Rapids, Michigan / Cambridge, U.K.

Wm. B. Eerdmans Publishing Co.
255 Jefferson Ave. S.E., Grand Rapids, Michigan 49503 /
P.O. Box 163, Cambridge CB3 9PU U.K.
www.eerdmans.com

Printed in the United States of America

07 06 05 04 03 02   7 6 5 4 3 2 1

Library of Congress Cataloging-in-Publication Data

Gross, Nancy Lammers, 1956-
If you cannot preach like Paul . . . / Nancy Lammers Gross.
p.   cm.
Includes bibliographical references.
ISBN 0-8028-4938-5 (pbk.: alk. paper)
1. Bible. N.T. Epistles of Paul — Homiletical use.
I. Title: If you cannot preach like Paul. . . .   II. Title.

BS26550.55.G76   2002
227′.06 — dc21

2001058450

Epigraph from "There is a Balm in Gilead" by William L. Dawson.
Published by Neil A. Kjos Music Co., Park Ridge, IL, 1939.

Contents

Acknowledgments

Bringing forth this book has been a journey on which I have been accompanied by the saints, a great cloud of witnesses. Because the book deals with themes that go back to my earliest days of thinking consciously about my faith, it is in some ways a very personal book. We all have stories from our formative years that are integral to the development of our faith convictions and our thinking. It has been a blessing to revisit many of my growing-up stories through the writing of this book, both the painful and the happy, because through them all God has worked for good. I am immeasurably grateful.

Even before my reflective thinking skills began emerging as an early adolescent, I was formed in the faith by my parents, who presented me for baptism when I was six weeks old, ingrained in my brothers and me a pattern of prayer, and kept me in the church all the years of my childhood. I am grateful to them, John V. Lammers and Elnor R. Lammers, for their faithfulness.

I was nurtured in the faith as I was growing up by three congregations: the First Presbyterian Churches of St. Charles, Missouri; Glen Ellyn, Illinois; and Burlingame, California. I am grateful to the witness of these congregations and for their shared commitment to the promises made to me in St. Charles on the day of my baptism: that they would be for me the people of God, telling me the story of Jesus, showing me the love of God and nurturing me in the faith until the day when I could stand and claim it for my own. I remember them with gratitude every time I make those promises on behalf of another child being baptized.

Some of the core ideas found in this book were conceived during the days of my Ph.D. program at Princeton Theological Seminary. I am grateful to Ann Hoch and Nora Tubbs Tisdale who shared the journey with me in those days and in the days since; to Kendy McCloskey Easley and Dayle Gillespie Rounds, sisters who have long sustained me on the journey; and to Thomas G. Long who not only helped me to give focus and language to some of the core ideas in this book, but encouraged me to write the book as well.

My students at the Eastern Baptist Theological Seminary have been an integral part of my growing up as a teacher, and I am very grateful to them. Nina Peck Reeder was an enormously able research assistant for this project during her senior year at Eastern Seminary. Her able and critical eye was a significant help in refining these pages.

I am grateful to the Board of Trustees of Eastern Seminary for the sabbatical leave in which to pursue this project, and for their forward thinking to grant such benefits to regular faculty persons who work less than full time. Their progressive policies have allowed this mother of young children both to pursue her ministry and spend significant time at home.

The administration and faculty of Eastern Seminary have been wonderful colleagues and friends for the journey. Thank you to former President (and still James A. Maxwell Professor of Biblical Theology) Manfred T. Brauch, President R. Scott Rodin, and Dean Eric H. Ohlmann for supporting my sabbatical leave. Manfred Brauch also read every page and gave me important feedback on the book. I am grateful for the support and friendship of Melody Mazuk, our library director, and Elouise Renich Fraser, professor of systematic theology. Of no small import was Elouise's early encouragement and conversations in the formation of this book.

Princeton Theological Seminary has given invaluable institutional support. As a visiting lecturer in speech communication during the writing of this book, I had a small office in which I spent my sabbatical days absorbed in the three "r's": reading, writing, and ruminating. Dr. Charles L. Bartow, chairperson of the speech area, has been a wonderful mentor and colleague, and read through the entire manuscript twice, giving invaluable comment. He also suggested the title of the book. Lois Haydu, secretary of the speech and preaching areas, has been supportive on days when the walls were closing in and a big help in countless ways. Together Dr. Bartow and Ms. Haydu left the door open to invaluable office benefits. G. Robert Jacks has been an invaluable friend, colleague, mentor, and cheerleader. My office mate, Michael Hegeman, was not only a valued conversation partner, but those conversations were materially helpful to the book as well.

I am grateful to Heather Faller, my research assistant at Princeton Seminary, who gave an able critical eye to the final proofs of the book and assembled the index. Jennifer Hoffman, Associate Managing Editor at Eerdmans, was very gracious and helpful in shepherding the book through the final stages of publication.

I am an intellectual and spiritual child of the First Presbyterian Church of Burlingame and Dr. Thomas W. Gillespie, whose preaching ministry there from 1966 through 1983 was instrumental in my formation as a person and a person of faith. When young people of my generation were staying away from the church in droves, many of us were returning to Burlingame to hear the word preached in a lively and compelling way. Through Dr. Gillespie's preaching ministry it became clear that all of life was subject to the gospel, and that there was nothing that could not or should not be brought into the captivity of the Lordship of Jesus Christ: not a book, idea, realm of human life, emotion, theory, philosophy, current event, or cultural norm. We heard the gospel engaged in and with contemporary life and it was life transforming. I was not alone. Sixteen of us from Burlingame during Dr. Gillespie's tenure responded to some form of call to ministry, eight women and eight men. It is my fondest hope that this book would honor the ministry of Dr. Gillespie and Mrs. Barbara Lugenbill Gillespie, and it is to that end that this book is dedicated.

Finally, I cannot conceive the journey without the companionship of my family. The sabbatical year was rich because in many ways I had more time for family, not less. Our daughters, Anna Catherine and Abby Louise, are to me light and life, and through them the goodness of God is manifest daily. My husband, John Robert Gross, is my rock.

His steadfastness, love, humor, and music make life rich beyond imagination. John and the girls make my joy complete.

Nancy Lammers Gross
Princeton, New Jersey

Introduction

Twice in Philippians Paul encourages the Christians at Philippi to imitate him: "Brothers and sisters, join in imitating me, and observe those who live according to the example you have in us" (3:17) and "Keep on doing the things that you have learned and received and heard and seen in me, and the God of peace will be with you" (4:9). In 1 Corinthians, Paul says, "Be imitators of me, as I am of Christ" (11:1).

In many respects this is scandalous. Paul has been accused of everything from patriarchalism and chauvinism to being a misogynist and a racist. Why would we imitate him? Pauline texts are often at the center of theo-political debates in the church today. Why would we keep doing the things Paul did? It might be considered especially scandalous that a woman would propose imitating Paul and doing the things he did. This book and the preaching that I hope it engenders, however, rest on the singular conviction that the cross of Christ is the only scandal with which we need to concern ourselves, and that the fear of all other human scandals dare not impede our preaching of Jesus Christ and him crucified.

My purpose is quite simple and without political position or rancor. My purpose is to reclaim Paul for the preaching ministry of the church.

I believe Paul has fallen out of favor in the church, especially in the pulpit, because preachers are genuinely confused as to how to navigate the confusing waters of Paul's letters. The treatment of Paul in homiletical texts has been spotty or brief at best, and homiletical books specifically addressing how to preach from Paul have been few and far between. Biblical theology books on Paul are often not helpful either because they do not lend themselves to conclusions on homiletical matters, or because they weigh theological matters in such a scholarly, academic fashion that many pastors find these treatises too distant from the business of the pulpit to be useful, even if they do get around to reading them.

The homiletical trend of the last twenty-five years, from which we are only just now emerging, has been narrative preaching. After generations of "three points and a poem," the pendulum swung far in the other direction and the narrative movement caught nearly every preacher's attention and imagination. According to conventional wisdom, the Pauline epistles clearly do not lend themselves to narrative preaching.[1] This, coupled with the increased use of the Common and now the Revised Common Lectionary, with semi-continuous readings from the synoptic Gospels serving to organize the weekly texts, has led to further disuse of the Pauline epistles as primary preaching texts.

It was not simply the wave of narrative preaching or the use of the lectionary that swept us away from Pauline preaching, however. The Pauline epistles have genuinely been misused, and congregations abused, by wayward preaching that purportedly was inspired by a Pauline text. The Pauline epistles have invited many, especially those of Western European descent, to create and preach systems in which some classes of people are more privileged than others. Pauline writings were, in fact, used to keep African slaves in their place in America, and women have been silenced in the churches — all using Paul as a rationale. The Pauline epistles have invited many to make firm, inflexi-

---

1. As long as the preacher seeks to form the sermon in a way coherent with the form of the biblical text, or the genre, the Pauline epistles will not be conducive to narrative preaching. But the sermon that arises from a Pauline text may have as its deep structure a narrative plot form. In plot form the sermon may not be a story, per se, but may move like a plot. Similarly, the sermon may not be in plot form but may communicate through a series of stories. Gene Lowry has been helpful in thinking about what actually makes a narrative sermon narrative.

ble decisions regarding the application of the gospel without understanding what to make of the space between the horizon of Paul's writing and the horizon of our living. Paul's letters are so specific in their address to pastoral situations, it became inevitable that when removing what Paul said from the socio-religious context in which he said it, the message could be distorted and used as a battering ram, rather than leading to a faithful word.

Another reason preaching from the Pauline epistles has fallen out of favor is that even when it was done reasonably well, the sermons tended to be explanations of theological doctrines or concepts derived from Paul. There is a sense in which we have heard it all before and explained it all before, and yet having these right answers has not always led us to the abundant life.[2] Preaching from Paul has tended to suit our heads, but not advanced the cause of claiming our hearts. It has made the distance between head and heart, of which Fred Craddock speaks — a distance every person must travel — even greater.[3] This has led to the impression that Paul was the logical apostle without passion.

Robert Jewett reports that when he traveled for a year on sabbatical he noticed a paucity of preaching from Paul. When he asked preachers why they avoided Paul, he got complaints about the "difficult Paul." Confusion reigned regarding how to communicate to a congregation the argumentative nature of Paul's letters. In many Protestant and Reformed churches he found the preaching of Paul mostly limited to three occasions: "On Reformation Sunday (Rom. 1:16-17), for weddings (1 Cor. 13) and for funerals (Rom. 8:31-39)!"[4]

Still further, many have not been preaching from Paul out of sheer confusion over what to make of Paul's apparent turn from preaching the Kingdom of God, as Jesus did, to preaching Jesus. In an age of so-

---

2. See Fred B. Craddock, *Overhearing the Gospel* (Nashville: Abingdon Press, 1978), and his reference to Søren Kierkegaard: "There is no lack of information in a Christian land; something else is lacking, and this is a something which the one man cannot directly communicate to the other" (p. 9).

3. Fred B. Craddock, *As One Without Authority* (Nashville: Abingdon Press, 1971), p. 78.

4. Robert Jewett, *Paul: The Apostle to America* (Louisville: Westminster/John Knox Press, 1994), p. 14.

cial concern and unrest it seemed more Christlike to preach the Kingdom of God and our responsibility for it than to preach personal salvation. Somehow Paul's preaching of Jesus got pitted against Jesus' preaching the Kingdom. Many have reacted against the singular, narrow, evangelistic preaching of Paul's Jesus to the exclusion of preaching the Kingdom of God.

Preachers are right to seek a balance. Throwing out Paul altogether is not the answer, however, especially since the distortions can be corrected. After all, Jesus did not preach only the Kingdom of God. Jesus also said, "Come to me, all you that are weary and are carrying heavy burdens, and I will give you rest" (Matt. 11:28) and "I am the way, and the truth, and the life" (John 14:6). Alternatively, Paul did not only preach Jesus for personal salvation. Paul was also concerned about stewardship and the poor (2 Cor. 8), and with the radical equality of all persons before Christ (Gal. 3:28).

The apostolic context demanded the preaching of Jesus. When Jesus was crucified, dead, and buried, and then raised again, God said "Yes!" to the ministry of Jesus (2 Cor. 1:19, 20). The subject did not change from the Kingdom of God, but expanded to lead with the preaching of Jesus when Jesus returned and commanded his disciples, "Go therefore and make disciples of all nations, baptizing them in the name of the Father and of the Son and of the Holy Spirit and teaching them to observe all that I have commanded you" (Matt. 28:18).

N. T. Wright has made the case that if Paul had simply parroted Jesus, repeating Jesus' parables, trying to do again what Jesus did in announcing and inaugurating the Kingdom, Paul would not have been endorsing Jesus; he would have been denying him. In effect, Paul would have been taking on the role of a would-be Messiah.

Jesus believed it was his vocation to bring Israel's history to its climax. Paul believed that Jesus had succeeded in that aim. Paul believed, in consequence of that belief and as part of his own special vocation, that he was himself now called to announce to the whole world that Israel's history had been brought to its climax in that way. *When Paul announced 'the gospel' to the Gentile world, therefore, he was deliberately and consciously implementing the achievement of Jesus*. He was, as he himself said, building on the foundation, not laying another one (1 Corinthians 3:11). He was not 'founding a separate religion.' He was not inventing a new ethical system. He was not perpetrating a timeless scheme of salvation, a new mystery-religion divorced from the real, human Jesus of Nazareth. He was calling the world to allegiance to its rightful Lord, the Jewish Messiah now exalted as the Jewish Messiah was always supposed to be.

. . . Jesus was not announcing 'a new religion'; nor was Paul . . . [t]he claim of Israel always was, the message of Jesus always was, and the announcement of Paul always was, that the human race was to be shown, invited to, summoned into, and enabled to discover the true way of being human, the way to reflect the very image of God himself in every aspect of life and with every fibre of one's being. If that is what you mean by 'religion', so be it. Jesus and Paul thought of it as Life, as being human, as being the children of God.

When all this is said and done, it should be comparatively easy to work through the actions and message of Jesus, and the agenda and letters of Paul, and to show that there is between them, not (of course) a one-for-one correspondence, but a coherence, an appropriate correlation, an integration that allows fully for the radically different perspective of each. Jesus was bringing Israel's history to its climax; Paul was living in the light of that climax.[5]

Paul did not trump Jesus' concern for the Kingdom of God. Paul was being faithful to Jesus' command to tend the sheep, to make disciples, to invite all persons into the Kingdom of God and to prepare for the Kingdom in its future manifestation.

Put more simply, Jesus' preaching of the Kingdom and Paul's preaching of Jesus have been pitted against each other as social concern preaching versus evangelical preaching. This is a dichotomy not present in the New Testament. Personal accountability before God and the love of God through Jesus are present in the Gospels. Social context and concern are present in the Pauline epistles. We need to find a way to strengthen this correlation within our contemporary preaching.

---

5. N. T. Wright, *What Saint Paul Really Said: Was Paul of Tarsus the Real Founder of Christianity?* (Grand Rapids: Eerdmans, 1997), pp. 180-82.

We must preach not only the Kingdom of God, but also Jesus; not only Jesus, but also the Kingdom of God. It is important to reclaim Paul for the preaching ministry of the church because without a vital preaching presence emerging from the Pauline epistles, we are depriving the church of the whole counsel of God.[6] It is truly that simple. It is time to take what we know biblically and theologically, and train a new hermeneutic on the epistles of Paul for the proclamation of the gospel for today.

Chapter one begins with my own experience in coming to grips with how to preach from Paul — I had always been convinced that faithful preaching from Paul works; I just didn't know why or how. Then we turn to a brief historical overview of the dominant ways in which Paul has been used in preaching, and the problematic ways Paul is typically preached today. Finally we will look at three homiletical treatments of preaching Paul from the last fifteen years or so — Daniel Patte in *Preaching Paul* (Philadelphia: Fortress Press, 1984); David Buttrick in *Homiletic: Moves and Structures* (Philadelphia: Fortress Press, 1987), and Thomas G. Long in *Preaching and the Literary Forms of the Bible* (Philadelphia: Fortress Press, 1989). These three contributions to homiletical method in dealing with Pauline texts for preaching provide important insights that will inform our approach. They will also assist us in clarifying the questions that still need to be asked.[7]

The second chapter will engage the assistance of scholars from systematic, biblical, and practical theological circles in coming to a new understanding of who Paul was and what his ministry was about. Traditionally, Paul has been treated as a systematic theologian, and his epistles as doctrinal treatises. Therefore the Pauline corpus has given rise to preaching that is most commonly an explication of theological doctrine, rather than a dialogue between the gospel and the contempo-

---

6. "The Westminster Confession of Faith," *The Constitution of the Presbyterian Church (U.S.A.) Part I, The Book of Confessions* (Louisville: The Office of the General Assembly, 1991), C.6006, p. 127.

7. See also James W. Thompson, *Preaching Like Paul: Homiletical Wisdom for Today* (Louisville: Westminster/John Knox Press, 2001). Unfortunately, Thompson's book was published too recently to be considered in this work.

rary situation. We will uncover the historical development of this tradition and propose a new way of viewing Paul as a practical theologian. If we are to do as Paul did and not just say what he said, we need a new vision of what it was he did.

The third chapter will effect a paradigm shift in the way we think about hermeneutics, the business of interpretation, and homiletics, the business of preaching. We will lay a new hermeneutical foundation for treating Paul in which homiletics becomes the last step in the hermeneutical process, rather than hermeneutics being a step in the middle of the homiletical process. In fact, this new hermeneutical foundation is valid not only for preaching from Paul, but for all preaching for those who attribute to scripture authority for matters of life and faith. In many respects this hermeneutical approach for biblical preaching provides a solution to one of the vexing problems with issues of interpretation in preaching — what has traditionally been understood as the interpretive "step" which takes preachers over the "chasm" between work with the biblical text and the preaching of the sermon.

The fourth chapter will describe the new homiletic, a hermeneutical methodology for preaching from Paul. Using Acts 20:7-12, the story of the night Paul preached until dawn and Eutychus fell out of a third-story window, we will walk through the method. Using a Luke-Acts story to demonstrate my method for preaching from Paul does beg the obvious question, "Why not use a Pauline text?" After pondering this question myself, I decided to use the Eutychus story for these reasons:

1. I am not only a homiletician, I am a preacher. Being too self-aware of one's homiletical process is a sure-fire way to make sure "the preacher" never comes, as they say in the African American church. In retrospect, I was able to catch myself in the act of committing my method most fully in the Eutychus sermon.
2. The Eutychus text was compelling for preaching, but not because of the obvious facts of the story. The Eutychus text pointed beyond itself, as Ricoeur and Ebeling discuss, in a most profound way, further illustrating the method.
3. In an important sense, the Eutychus sermon *is* a Pauline sermon.

One could cynically suggest that I merely conjectured what Paul might have been saying to the Christians in Troas. Nevertheless, it was Paul who was preaching and it made sense to suggest that he preached from his own thinking, writing, and convictions.

4. Finally, I do claim that the method is valid for all biblical preaching, not just preaching from Paul. Since I am concerned to add my voice to the dialogue regarding how we treat Paul in the pulpit, this book consequently has as its special emphasis preaching from Paul. The emphasis on Paul, however, should not be interpreted to mean that there will be great divergence from these methodological convictions when preaching other biblical genre.

The fifth chapter presents the Eutychus sermon and two other sermons that emerged from Pauline texts. While not going into the same degree of detail as the Eutychus sermon preparation process, I give not only the context that gave rise to the sermons, but also the major concerns and questions that arose from the texts and that pointed to the direction the sermons would take.

CHAPTER ONE

Endgame

I grew up listening to preaching that came from the Pauline epistles. My experience of that preaching was that the gospel was clear. I was named as Christ's person, I was called as Jesus' disciple, God in Christ found me and found me out. I knew that God knew me. Between the prayer of confession and the preaching of the gospel, often based on a Pauline text, I felt as though my life was an open book. I wondered then how a preacher who didn't know me personally, a prayer of confession written by someone else and prayed corporately, and a service of worship attended by three hundred other people could speak so directly to the confusion of my early adolescent life. Throughout my early years, the strength of my convictions developed through participation in corporate worship together with the confusion of adolescent life combined to create in me an urgency that was later expressed through ordained ministry.

Life was not easy for me in my early adolescent years. It seemed to me that my family life was not very happy. Something I could not name was deeply wrong and it troubled me. I was overweight and prone to depression. I wanted to hide. I also wanted desperately to be found. This led to the confounding situation of wanting and needing the gospel, while at the same time rejecting the efforts of the elders of my church to reach out to me.[1] When I went to church I tried to hide.

---

1. I still recall Gordon Bell and another elder visiting me in my home and trying

But from God there was no hiding. It seemed that the gracious love of God and the good news of Jesus Christ constantly reached into the deepest hiding place and met me there. The gospel brought perspective to my life, and an answer bigger than all of my questions. I became vividly aware that Jesus Christ was my only hope in the world, and that only through the gospel of Jesus Christ could I hope to make sense of my world. I was fourteen years old.

The gospel of Jesus Christ was so big for me, I thought I should be one of those who preached it. Surely there could be nothing more profoundly worthwhile to do in life than to be a preacher. I found the moment and meaning of the call to worship so significant, so weighty, I believed I had to do the calling. If it was this important for me, how could I consider doing anything else in life? I had no idea what this meant and had no language for understanding a call to ordained ministry. I was a girl. I had never seen a woman pastor. I could not even begin to fathom how to get from adolescence to the pulpit. It seemed an impossible journey.

I used to wonder where sermons came from. I was amazed that our pastor got up and brought forth these words — this Word — week after week. I played the saxophone in a variety of Junior High and High School bands. I was especially talented at reading music. Becoming highly proficient at sight reading music, I could read nearly any rhythm our Jazz Band Director presented us, including those intended to stump us. What stumped *me* was the improvisation that is expected of any jazz saxophone player. I would go into a state of near paralysis when confronted with sixty-four bars of chords where my sax solo was supposed to be. I understood the chords. I knew the theory. I simply didn't have the music inside me. Or, if I did have it inside me, it was so buried beneath layers of self-consciousness, self-doubt, and fear it did not have even the most remote chance of surfacing.

I used to wonder how I could ever preach if I couldn't improvise a solo on my saxophone. There was an element of creativity and self-

---

to draw me back when I had dropped out of the youth group. I was barely polite to them in my rejection. I know Gordon's prayers for me over the years were honored by God, and I trust he is enjoying now his heavenly reward.

revelation involved that I did not believe I possessed. Playing jazz solos required a measure of self-knowledge and a confidence that what I had to play would be of interest to others. I possessed neither the self-knowledge nor the self-confidence. This was not a *sub*-conscious thought. Before I put out of my mind for nearly four years the inner compulsion to call people to worship and preach the gospel, I explicitly asked myself and pondered these very questions. If I couldn't improvise on the saxophone, how could I ever create a sermon?

Finally, I attributed to girlhood fantasizing the inner compulsion to call and to preach and shelved it in the recesses of my imagination. Perhaps the final blow to any possibility for understanding myself as a minister was the mistaken impression that you had to go to a "cemetery" for school, and I simply couldn't envision myself walking among gravestones wearing a black Geneva gown! What a frightening adolescent image for life at seminary. No doubt this walk through the graveyard would be in an atmospheric and spiritual fog, not unlike the fog through which Richard Todd stumbled early in the movie *A Man Called Peter,* a movie which had further galvanized my ill-defined sense of purpose.

To all outward appearances my life took the path of a straight arrow. I went straight from high school to college and from college straight to seminary. Internally, however, my journey took anything but a straight arrow trajectory. I was admitted to college on the strength of my music performance with virtually no confidence that I had what it took to succeed academically. My studies were motivated by a fear of failure and being kicked out of school. After securing my academic place in the institution by successfully completing one semester of the music program, including the music theory course that effectively weeded out the weaker students, I wandered from philosophy to religion and finally to political theory for an intellectual home. My advisor and major professor wondered aloud to me if I was one of those people who never stayed with anything for long, but would always be a sojourner looking for the next challenge. I knew even then I was on a journey, but the question haunted me.

Nobody in my dormitory went to church voluntarily, so far as I could tell. There were a number of us, however, who sang in the Methodist church choir because our music theory professor was the director. He told us unabashedly that we would get brownie points for coming to sing with his small church choir. This accomplished my need to get to church without looking too religious (and my need to pass music theory!), but worship there was too different from what I knew at home. It did not satisfy my deep spiritual longings. The next year I found that when I went to the Presbyterian church, if I sat at the back and slipped out of service a little early, I could get back to my dorm room to change clothes and still make it to the cafeteria for lunch. I wouldn't have dreamed of going to lunch in my church clothes. The potential derision of my hall mates was more than I could dare to withstand.

Finally, the summer after my sophomore year in college, I had to confront what I knew only as the fantasy of a fourteen-year-old, and which now resurfaced as the singular vision that got in the way of anything else I tried to do. I had already written letters and made several visits to my home pastor through those first two years of college, but never had the courage to confess what was hidden deep in my heart. At Christmas of my junior year, I told my pastor of this sense of purpose for which I still had no language. I was surprised to hear he already knew, and was simply waiting for me to come to grips with the call that had been placed upon me. The language had always been there; I just couldn't hear it because I had never dreamed it could apply to me. No one had ever told me I could not be a preacher. Neither had anyone ever told me I could. When I first came upon 1 Corinthians 9:16, "If I proclaim the gospel, this gives me no ground for boasting, for an obligation is laid on me, and woe to me if I do not preach the gospel!", I recognized it immediately as an expression of my own experience and call.

Through it all, I found myself blessed with faith resources to sustain me on the journey and an inarticulate, yet growing, theological framework from which to process my journey. My constant and my anchor was this preaching from Paul, my reading holy Scripture as I found it in the Pauline epistles, and the theological tradition that had already deeply and even subconsciously formed me, and for which I found a language in Paul.[2]

2. In my search for a way to interpret the events of my life, I expressed questions

When I arrived at seminary, I was stunned to find that many of my fellow students hated Paul. Late night dormitory conversations revealed that many would not even preach from Paul, finding the narratives of Old and New Testaments so much more rich. Still further, it seemed that many were completely baffled by *how* to preach from Paul. The narratives give a story to tell, a natural structure to the sermon. What is there to do with Paul but simply to repeat what he said? And how do you do that when so much of what Paul said was intolerably offensive? These were questions I had never heard nor asked. My confidence in the liberating word of Jesus Christ was always bigger than the difficult issues found in the Pauline corpus.

In some ways I've been waiting all my life to write this book. My early questions — where does the sermon come from, and how can I preach if I cannot improvise on the sax? — were tamed by the discovery that God gives the utterance through the witness and guidance of Scripture in the power of the Holy Spirit. I thought I was all alone on my saxophone. In my preaching I was attended by the one who is called Word. Later, my work in doctoral seminars and the direction of my dissertation were motivated by the questions, *why* does preaching work and *how* does it work? This led me into hermeneutical studies, and eventually in my teaching to a more focused study on preaching from the Pauline epistles.

Layers of complication exist now that were not so clearly an issue thirty years ago. Theo-political battles have raged for decades over feminist, hierarchical, patriarchal, and sexuality issues. While these issues were alive in the academy thirty years ago, they had not yet shaped much of the preaching in the country. Today it is hard for a preacher *not* to feel that preaching from Paul indicates some kind of political endorsement of Paul. How can we preach the foundational kerygmatic themes from Paul, such as salvation by grace through faith and the resurrection of Jesus Christ from the dead, without de facto

---

to a youth pastor who told me that I "should read the New Testament." Not knowing where to begin, I started with the Gospel of Matthew and was immediately hung up by the genealogies. When I got to the birth narrative, it was not the account with which I had become familiar, and so I returned again to the Pauline passages from which the pastor had recently preached.

endorsing everything Paul says? How do we deal with the more offensive aspects of Pauline letters which some scholars reject as inauthentic, when some of the clearest kerygmatic statements are made in the same letters?[3] And if we cannot endorse everything Paul says, then how can we trust the foundational kerygmatic themes? And finally, if we ever settle for ourselves the troubling issues of what to preach from Paul, we run headlong into the question of how to do it. Is preaching the kerygmatic themes we distill from Paul what we are supposed to preach when working from a Pauline text? Or is there still another way?

The clues as to what we preach and how to preach it when dealing with the Pauline epistles must begin with Paul. If we look to Paul and ask ourselves the question, how did Paul begin?, we will find that often Paul began with what I call the "Endgame."

3. The question of Pauline authorship of letters such as Colossians and Ephesians, not raised until the rise of biblical criticism in the nineteenth century, is still debated today. That Paul *did not* perhaps write these letters has been, for some, reason not to preach from them. The offensive parts of these letters may then be dismissed as the wanderings of a misguided disciple of Paul. There is strong support, however, for affirming Pauline authorship, especially for Colossians. See, e.g., F. F. Bruce, *The Epistles to the Colossians, to Philemon, and to the Ephesians,* The New International Commentary on the New Testament (Grand Rapids: Eerdmans, 1984); Craig Keener, *The IVP Bible Background Commentary: New Testament* (Downers Grove, IL: InterVarsity Press, 1993); and *A Dictionary of Paul and His Letters: A Compendium of Contemporary Biblical Scholarship* (Downers Grove, IL: InterVarsity Press, 1993). My own biblical theological and hermeneutical assumptions, operative in this book, affirm canonical hermeneutics, where greater emphasis is placed on the final form of the text than on the stages of development that led to the final text. "In interpreting the text [from this perspective], readers must ask not only historical and literary questions about the text, but also how and why the text has addressed communities of faith. Their canonical status means that the texts have acquired a universal audience — communities of faith in every age and place who read them not simply to ask what their original authors intended but what they are saying to the living community of faith in the present." *Harper's Bible Dictionary,* Paul J. Achtemeier, ed. (San Francisco: Harper & Row, 1985), p. 133.

Endgame

I have been intrigued by the term "endgame" since an August 1998 issue of *U.S. News and World Report* with the front cover screaming, "Starr's Endgame," came into the house. "Endgame" refers to final, critical moves. It has a rich history in the play of chess and bridge, and in the description of the final moves in battle to bring a conflict to an end. It has become a popular term for anything that has been a protracted or conflictual issue and seems finally to be coming to an end.

I confess that even though the game of chess is played with pieces named for figures involved in medieval combat, I had never associated chess with warfare. I had associated the play of chess with mighty brains, not mighty muscles, though often with the brains came the warring temperament of genius.

Imagine my surprise to walk into one of the ubiquitous McDonald's on Interstate 95 somewhere in Connecticut in order to take a little daughter to one of countless bathroom stops, and finding six brawny men, several in tank tops with bulging shoulders — Hispanic, black, and white — sitting over plastic chess mats with a timer at each table, moving pieces swiftly and decisively, and hammering their respective timer buttons with the intensity of a Shaquille O'Neill slam dunk. They knew about endgames.

It is amazing who has an endgame these days. Scan the newspapers, magazines, and journals from the last twenty-four months and you will discover an endgame in Detroit,[4] Kosovo,[5] and North Korea.[6] There is an endgame in Indonesia,[7] the Mideast,[8] and in the Cold War with German Reunification.[9]

---

4. *Columbia Journalism Review* 36, no. 3 (September/October 1997): 20. This article reports a judgment finding several Detroit newspapers guilty of unfair labor practices.

5. *Christian Science Monitor,* 1 June 1999, p. 6.

6. *Wall Street Journal,* 27 February 1997, Eastern edition.

7. *Asiaweek,* 29 October 1999, p. 14.

8. *The New York Times,* 6 April 1997.

9. *International Security,* Spring 1997, p. 159.

Intel has keyed in on a wireless endgame;[10] Microsoft has been involved in a high-stakes antitrust endgame;[11] and there has been an endgame in the financial services industry in the United States banking industry.[12] Apparently there is an "Endgame of Sexual Liberalism."[13] Unfortunately there is reportedly an endgame for girls because the game of chess remains mystifyingly male-dominated and oddly segregated.[14] There is even an endgame being played out in the discussion of methods for studying protein-protein interactions.[15]

More profoundly, "Endgame" was the name of a one-act play by Nobel Prize-winning Irish playwright Samuel Beckett. First published in Paris in 1957, *Endgame* is a tragicomedy combining the bleakest of human predicaments with penetrating humor. The characters themselves use their own pains to entertain themselves. The play shows how desperately we need each other, especially at the end of our lives, and how we both hope for and dread further development in our lives.[16]

The apostle Paul's endgame is about the end of time as we know it. Paul's endgame is about the "day of our Lord" (2 Cor. 1:14), the "day of Jesus Christ" (Phil. 1:6), the "day of our Lord Jesus Christ" (1 Cor. 1:8). Paul's endgame is about "the end" (1 Cor. 1:8); it is about the "fullness of time" (Eph. 1:10). It is also about the "wrath that is coming" (1 Thess. 1:10), and therefore the Christ who came for us, who continues to beckon us, who stands for us as the pioneer and perfecter of our faith. The endgame is still about the "Jesus who rescues us" (1 Thess. 1:10). For Paul the endgame is the apocalypse, and how we live in the end time.

10. *PC Week,* 3 January 2000, p. 14.

11. *Wall Street Journal,* 10 November 1999, Eastern edition.

12. *McKinsey Quarterly,* no. 4 (1997): 170.

13. *American Enterprise* 8, no. 6 (November/December 1997): 14. This article reports the U.S. District Court judge's ruling on the case of Bob Guccione Jr., son of the founder of *Penthouse.* It gives the judge's finding on the conditions of the job benefits at *Spin* magazine after hearing from witnesses.

14. *The New York Times,* 19 December 1996.

15. *Science,* 18 June 1999, p. 1948.

16. I am indebted to Robert Lanchester of Princeton Theological Seminary for this synopsis.

Paul's goal is that "we should bring about the obedience of faith among all the Gentiles for the sake of Jesus' name" (Rom. 1:5). Paul's goal is that we should stand "blameless on the day of our Lord Jesus Christ" (1 Cor. 1:8). Paul knows that the one who began a good work in us will bring it to completion by the day of Jesus Christ (Phil. 1:6). For Paul the day of our Lord can be characterized by the term "endgame" because it reflects an imminent end. His letters, at least his earlier letters, bear the character of final communications as to how the end should be played out.[17]

The curious thing about Paul's endgame, however, is that he so often *begins* with it. 1 Corinthians, 2 Corinthians, and Philippians clearly begin with a strong reference to the endgame, the day of Jesus Christ. More subtle references to the endgame are made at the beginning of other letters.

Paul's proclivity for beginning with the endgame sheds light on an important aspect of Paul's theology and methodology. In a sense the beginning and ending of his letters, the parts which often concern the endgame, serve as two handles of a basket. I am indebted to my German tutor for this image. In trying to explain to me the inscrutable mysteries of German syntax, Mrs. Froehlich likened a German sentence to a basket. The verbs at the beginning and at the end of the sentence are the handles to the basket. And inside the basket you can put all kinds of wonderful things!

Proclamations about the endgame are like the handles of the baskets of Paul's letters. And inside the baskets we find all kinds of won-

---

17. The centrality of Jewish apocalyptic thought to Paul's gospel is well documented by biblical theologians. J. Christiaan Beker suggests that "Jewish apocalyptic is the substratum and master symbolism of Paul's thought because it constituted the linguistic world of Paul the Pharisee and therefore formed the indispensable filter, context, and grammar by which he appropriated and interpreted the Christ-event. . . ." Beker maintains that "apocalyptic *motifs* dominate Paul's thought, that Paul's modifications of the Christian tradition are *not* due to Hellenistic-Jewish or Philonic influences but are modifications of an apocalyptic substratum." J. Christiaan Beker, "Recasting Pauline Theology: The Coherence-Contingency Scheme as Interpretive Model," in *Pauline Theology, Vol. 1: Thessalonians, Philippians, Galatians, Philemon*, ed. Jouette M. Bassler (Minneapolis: Fortress Press, 1991), pp. 17, 18.

derful things! Paul's messages to Christians in Corinth and Philippi are explicitly bracketed by this clear reference to the endgame. Theologically you will find it in the other letters as well.

The day of our Lord Jesus is coming. Come, Lord, come. There is nothing foggy about this vision. It is crystal clear. There is nothing uncertain about our need not only to have faith in Jesus Christ, but to bring about the obedience of the Gentiles through faith. All this so that we may cooperate in the plan for the fullness of time, the plan to gather up all things into Christ who is the head. This is our certainty, the handles of the basket of the gospel given us by Paul: faith in Christ, and obedience to him who is and who was and who is to come. We begin and end with this confidence. This confidence serves as the handles of the basket.

The problem is with all the wonderful kinds of things inside the basket.

Many approach preaching with confidence in the handles. We have confidence in the Christ who is and who was, who will always be, and who is to come. Many of us, however, also have the stuff *inside* our baskets in order. Everything has its name and place and significance in life. This is often where the trouble begins.

Perhaps you grew up in a strong preaching tradition that taught you what all the hallmarks of faith mean. Perhaps you had a mentor who modeled for you all the right theological answers. Perhaps you grew up in a Christian community where the social order kept everyone in a clearly defined position and all knew their place. Perhaps you already know what the Bible means and what Scripture preaches, so to speak, and which kinds of sermons preach.

That is not a bad place to be. It is not bad to come to seminary or to leave seminary knowing who you are and what you believe, and having a strong foundation from which to grow.

The only problem is when we stay there. The only problem is when we refuse to look into that basket, and get out all the things that we have so carefully ordered in the basket. The problem comes when we refuse to let anyone else look in that basket or ask questions about what is in the basket. The problem is when we decide that the things in our baskets are the only right things to have in a pastoral or theological basket and when we insist that our way of packing them into the basket is the only right way of packing them. This is often what happens with preaching from the Pauline corpus. Creativity may abound in preaching from the Gospels or Old Testament narratives, or even the poetry of the Psalms. When we get to Paul, however, we tend to slide over into the answers, the doctrines, the explanations of theological terms, the system by which we order our faith seeking understanding.

Now, many of us might feel rather content with ourselves at this point, rather self-satisfied, saying, "Well, that's not me. I'm not that sure of myself, and I'm more flexible than that, after all. The only right answers are the ones I get from the Bible, and it is clear what the right answers are in the Bible."

I am fond of that section in the fifteenth chapter of 1 Corinthians where Paul is on a roll describing the endgame. Paul has been trying to establish the veracity of the resurrection of the dead, showing how you cannot believe in the resurrection of *Jesus Christ* from the dead if there is no *resurrection* of the dead and how if there is no *resurrection* of the dead and therefore no resurrection of *Jesus Christ* from the dead then our faith is in vain.

In 1 Corinthians 15:27 Paul says,

> For "God has put all things in subjection under his feet." But when it says *[see, we have a little exegesis going on here]*, "All things are put in subjection," it is plain that this does not include the one who put all things in subjection under him. When all things are subjected to him, then the Son himself will also be subjected to the one who put all things in subjection under him, so that God may be all in all.

While this sounds convoluted, and the simple reading of it may stump many in our congregations, it is actually not too difficult to figure out. Far more difficult is figuring out what from that passage ought to be preached, or if that passage ought to be preached at all. Far more difficult is figuring out what to do with that passage beyond explaining it. Even more troublesome still are the household codes, the *Haustafeln*, the relations between men and women, slave and free, Jew and Gentile, believer and unbeliever. Still more perplexing is how to live in the world but not of the world, or how to discern where love for our neighbor meets intolerable tolerance for "anything goes" behavior.

Far more difficult is hearing today a fresh word from the Lord through the apostle Paul when the world has changed so dramatically, while there is still "nothing new under the sun." The fact is, the stuff in the baskets of Paul's letters can be very messy. How do we deal with it?

I believe we find a clue in Paul's endgame. Paul begins Philippians with the endgame. He concludes it with this charge:

> Finally, beloved, whatever is true, whatever is honorable, whatever is just, whatever is pure, whatever is pleasing, whatever is commendable, if there is any excellence and if there is anything worthy of praise, think about these things. *Keep on doing* the things that you have learned and received and heard and seen in me, and the God of peace will be with you (4:8, 9).

Keep on doing the things that you have learned from me. Earlier in the letter Paul said, "Brothers and sisters, join in imitating me, and observe those who live according to the example you have in us" (3:17).

My proposal is simple:
Do what Paul did; don't just say what Paul said.

As preachers, we've been saying what Paul said for a long time. Saying what Paul said is a time-honored way of preaching. I have identified at least four ways of preaching from the Pauline corpus in which our primary method is to say what Paul said. Those four ways are:

- preaching Paul as though he was a *systematic theologian;*
- using Paul as a *proof text or launching pad;*
- deriving from a Pauline text a *kernel of truth;* and,
- preaching a *linear, rational deductive argument* using a Pauline text.

We have preached Paul as though he was a *systematic theologian* who intended only to be doctrinal and whose writing was rigorously

12

and exclusively systematic in nature. This is an historic approach to preaching from Paul and we have inherited it honestly from the Reformers. A glance through the sermons of Martin Luther or John Calvin or John Knox will demonstrate the extent to which the Reformers' preaching was doctrinal and systematic. Here is one example from Martin Luther — an excerpt from a sermon on "The Method and Fruits of Justification," based on Galatians 4:1-7.

> This text touches the very pith of Paul's chief doctrine. The cause why it is well understood but by few, is, not that it is so obscure and difficult, but because there is so little knowledge of faith left in the world; without which it is not possible to understand Paul, who every where treats of faith with such earnestness and force. . . . First, therefore, we must understand the doctrine in which good works are set forth, far different from that which treats of justification; as there is a great difference between the substance and its working; between man and his work. Justification pertains to man, and not to works; for man is either justified and saved, or judged and condemned, and not works.[18]

The Reformers preached doctrinally and systematically from Paul because it was a practical matter of lived faith to do so. Speaking to matters of doctrine meant speaking to the critical issues of people's lives as they began to pull away from the Roman Church.

When *we* preach Paul as systematic theologian, however, we tend to preach the Reformers' interpretation of Paul. Many take the answers to the Reformers' questions and use that as a lens to reading Paul. With the Reformers' conclusions as our lens through which to read Paul, it is a temptation to preach Paul as though Paul has already thought through our contemporary issues and has the right answers to our questions.

Preaching Paul's answers, or sayings, is tricky, but remains popular. It usually leads to some creative wriggling out of tight places when Paul's answers are no longer tenable in today's world, and everyone

18. Clyde E. Fant, Jr., and William M. Pinson, Jr., eds., *Twenty Centuries of Great Preaching,* 13 vols. (Waco, Texas: Word Books, 1971), vol. 2, p. 53.

draws a different line regarding which of Paul's answers are right and which are wrong, which can be taken literally and which need a contortionist to understand. Our sensibilities are often pricked when preaching Paul as systematic theologian, but it is so deeply imbedded in the modern Protestant preaching tradition, we often don't even realize we are doing it.

A second way to preach by saying what Paul said is to use Paul as a *proof text*. Use an Old Testament or Gospel text as your primary preaching text, and then bring Paul in at the end as the final authoritative word to prove what the last twenty or thirty minutes have been about. Still again, Paul has been used as a proof text when a short, pithy statement from Paul is used to launch a topical sermon that explicates the event or addresses the occasion of the day. A masterful sermon by Henry Sloane Coffin demonstrates this way of preaching Paul. Prepared for All Saints' Day, the following excerpt and outline comes from a sermon entitled, "All the Saints Salute You," using that snippet of Scripture from 2 Corinthians 13:13. There is virtually nothing in the sermon that bears the context of the passage from which this simple sentence comes. There is a sense in which all of historical Christian and biblical tradition is the text for this sermon.

> In every age Christians seem to remain the "little flock" their Master called his first followers. The relatively small congregations of believers in Christ in our time — minorities still on any Sunday in most communities — need to keep in mind the impressive society of which we are part. On an All Saints' day there come to us out of every century and from all over this globe, and from the mysterious world beyond the grave, voices of comrades in Christ — "All the saints salute you."
>
> I Salute you with *sympathy*. . . .
> II Salute you with *their witness to the reality* of him whom they believed. . . .
> III Salute you with *guidance*. . . .
> IV Salute you with *expectation*. . . .
> V Salute you with *present fellowship*.[19]

19. Fant and Pinson, eds., *Twenty Centuries*, vol. 8, pp. 315-21.

14

So great is the depth and breadth of Coffin's grasp of both Scripture and history, this sermon is powerfully moving. The method, however, of using a short Pauline statement as launching pad or proof text is fraught with danger, and can be easily mishandled, particularly by those of us less learned in matters of faith than Dr. Coffin.

A third way to say what Paul said is to use a bit of one of Paul's letters as a kernel of truth. Sometimes this kernel is got at exegetically; just as often it stands on its own self-apparent meaning and exegesis is unnecessary because it is being used only as a kernel of thought to enable preachers to say what they want to say. The following excerpt is from a sermon on grieving in which the preacher leads the congregation through *ten* stages of grief.

> The question is often asked, Is it right for a Christian person to grieve? Or, How should a Christian person respond to the loss of something or someone very dear to him?
>
> There are eight words in the Scripture (1 Thess. 4:13) which are often misunderstood. "Grieve not as those who have no hope." As we have grown up in the Church I am sure that many of us have felt that we were taught that when a truly Christian person confronts a grief situation he ought not to grieve. It is as if we took these eight words and cut them down to two so that all we have left is an admonition, Grieve not.
>
> But this is certainly out of character with the stories of people found on the pages of Holy Scripture. As we look at both the Old Testament and the New Testament we find that strong men, brave men, the great leaders of the faith through the centuries, grieved, sorrowed, shed tears when there was cause to grieve and to sorrow. The Psalmist says, "My tears have been my food day and night." . . .
>
> [Numerous grief situations are cited]
>
> . . . So I would like to suggest that in this eight-word portion of the Scripture we put a comma after the first word, so that it now reads, "Grieve, not as those who have no hope" — but for goodness sake, grieve.
>
> [Ten stages of grief follow. The sermon concludes with quotations from the Psalms, then . . .]

So we say, "Grieve — not as those who have no hope," but grieve.[20]

In some ways this is an excellent pastoral sermon on grieving. It is also a classic and common way in which a kernel of Pauline thought is used to give pith and point to a sermon developed on grounds other than the text.

A fourth way to say what Paul said is to actually preach from a Pauline text, but preach in the *rational, linear, deductive* way that makes an argument and proves the case. Usually the case that is proven in the sermon is that our world is just like the first-century world and Paul was right. Typically this manifests itself in an expository sermon where the exegesis of the passage is being preached. In a classic sermon by Robert Candlish (1806-1873), the 1 Corinthians text to which I referred above is carefully explained.

> "Then they also which are fallen asleep in Christ are perished. If in this life only we have hope in Christ, we are of all men most miserable." — 1 Corinthians 15:18, 19.

> This is the climax and close of the apostle's argument concerning the resurrection, in its negative form. He reasons with the deniers of the possibility of a resurrection, after the manner of what is technically called in logic *reductio ad absurdum;* pointing out the conclusion in which their doctrine must, by a few short and necessary steps, inevitably land them. . . .

> Have you thought seriously of the bearing of your new belief on your Saviour's work, and on your own faith and hope? Study it, and look at it, in that light. Surely you must perceive, that at all events, and in the first place, it involves a denial of the resurrection of Christ. . . . Your doctrine, that there is no resurrection of the dead, with the ground on which you defend it, — the essential vileness of matter, and its incompatibility with a perfect state of being, — makes that impossible. Plainly, if there be no resurrection of the

20. "The Christian and Grief," by Granger E. Westberg, *Rockefeller Chapel Sermons of Recent Years,* compiled by Donovan E. Smucker (Chicago: The University of Chicago Press, 1967), pp. 177-87.

dead, Christ is not risen. Are you prepared to face such a result of your philosophy?[21]

Candlish goes on to build a rational argument, not unlike Paul's, for the reality of the resurrection of Jesus Christ from the dead and the consequences for humanity.

Preaching Paul as *systematic theologian;* using a Pauline text as *proof text or launching pad;* deriving a *kernel of truth* from a Pauline text; or preaching a *linear, rational, deductive* argument from a Pauline text are all popular and traditional ways of preaching Paul. And why not? Paul was in some sense doctrinal and systematic. ". . . [F]or by grace you have been saved through faith, and this is not your own doing; it is the gift of God . . ." (Eph. 2:8) is not a bad jumping-off place for a sermon and it *is* a kernel of truth. And all speech is linear, in part, and stories have a rational structure. These are all ways of saying what Paul said; of preaching what Paul preached.

The problem is that these four ways of saying what Paul said are so easily mishandled. It is so much easier when saying what Paul said to be true to an agenda that is not related to the intention of the biblical text. In addition, Paul never told us to say what he said. He did, however, instruct us to join in imitating him, to do the things he did, to do the things that we have learned and received and heard and seen in Paul. Doing as Paul did rather than saying what he said leads us on a search for a whole different methodology. What were the kinds of things Paul did?

Paul was an evangelist. He was a church planter, a missionary, a pastor. He was even an administrator of sorts, a head of staff, as he decided who should travel to which city as a part of the overall missionary effort. According to Johan Christiaan Beker, Paul was first and foremost an exegete.[22]

---

21. "The Pious Dead are Lost — Living Believers are Miserable," by Robert S. Candlish, *Great Sermons on the Resurrection of Christ, by Celebrated Preachers with Biographical Sketches and Bibliographies,* compiled by Wilbur M. Smith (Natick, MA: W. A. Wilde Co., 1964), pp. 235-45.

22. J. Christiaan Beker, *The Triumph of God: The Essence of Paul's Thought,* trans. Loren T. Stuckenbruck (Minneapolis: Fortress Press, 1990), p. 15.

Paul did not have a Pauline corpus from which to preach answers concerning the problems of his churches and budding Christian communities. Paul had a Scripture, the Hebrew Scriptures; and he had the gospel, the good news of Jesus Christ. This gospel was grounded in the Hebrew Scripture, was confirmed by the Holy Spirit, and very early on was testified to in the language we hear in 1 Corinthians 15:3ff.

> For I handed on to you as of first importance what I in turn had received: that Christ died for our sins in accordance with the Scriptures, and that he was buried, and that he was raised on the third day in accordance with the Scriptures, and that he appeared to Cephas, then to the twelve. Then he appeared to more than five hundred brothers and sisters at one time, most of whom are still alive, though some have died.

Paul was convinced to the core of his being that Jesus Christ was Lord, and that the cross of Christ stood at the crossroads of the two ages. Even though the apocalypse did not occur in the timely fashion Paul expected, the larger message throughout Paul's writings is that we stand at the juncture of the apocalypse, in every place and in every century. The crucifixion and resurrection of the one known as Jesus of Nazareth, the rending of the curtain, the quaking of the earth, and the stone rolled away are all markers of that place where the new age breaks in upon the old. The cross is the new lens. We cannot help but continue to look at the world with our old lenses, but the power of the cross is emptied if we do not view the world with "bifocals" or "stereoscopically."[23] Quoting James Kay,

---

23. James F. Kay, "The Word of the Cross at the Turn of the Ages," *Interpretation* 53 (January 1999): 44-56. This article is a succinct and fruitful analysis of the bind many contemporary preachers have in preaching a cross of Jesus which has come to represent so many ungodly, dehumanizing aspects of life and human history. While the cross has been used to justify such irredeemable practices as "enforced surrogacy imposed on African American women," rites of child sacrifice, ethnic cleansing, and the victimization of women who are encouraged to "take up their cross" at the expense of their own personhood, Kay brings "the word of the cross" back into proper relief as that which announces and sheds light on "God's invading and liberating new creation."

One of the reasons we preachers too readily retreat from apocalyptic conceptuality is that we continue to read this age only from its own point of view. Seeing only what the world sees, we end up saying nothing the world cannot say more eloquently to itself. We need bifocals! Our notions of "reality" are too flat, too linear, too unifocal; they remain trapped by *kata-sarka* canons. To take an example from Martyn, we often ask the question "Who killed Jesus?" Answers differ, but usually the Roman or Jewish authorities are named, with varying degrees of responsibility. Paul, by contrast, gives a bifocal answer: "The rulers of this age crucified the Lord of glory" (1 Cor. 2:8). That is, in the casualty on the apocalyptic battlefield at Calvary, God meets neither the Jews nor the Romans as such, but rather the power of evil, oppression, and dehumanization which acts in, through, and on these human agents and, indeed, all human beings. Thus, if we define "reality" nonapocalyptically, that is, by the norms of this age, we will miss what is really going on, because we are not *simultaneously* looking behind the scenes, between the lines, or under the surface. To preach the word of the cross in ways consistent with its apocalyptic context and content, we need to exchange our unifocal analogies, examples, and arguments for stereoscopic ones to see what God is up to in the world. Stereoscopic imagination can help the listener see the cruciform pattern of God's surprising work of redemption. But how does such imagination take rhetorical form? Or, in David Buttrick's words, how do we "paint the new creation on the wall of a condemned building"?[24]

Merely explaining Paul's words about the cross, or picking up one of Paul's phrases to use as a launching pad, proof text, or kernel of truth, is precisely too linear, too unifocal, trapped by *kata-sarka* vision and thought. It is precisely *not* preaching the word of the cross.

Paul lived out of the conviction that the God of the ancient and contemporary Hebrew people was also the God of the Gentiles. With the same passion that drove his persecution of the Christians earlier in his life, Paul was convinced that his ministry was to bring about the

24. Kay, "The Word of the Cross," p. 51.

faith and obedience of the Gentiles, to bring them to a life-giving knowledge of the Lordship of Jesus Christ.

Paul had these convictions, he had the Hebrew Scriptures and the testimony of the apostles and early believers, and he had his own experience of the resurrected Lord and this early creedal witness. This is essentially what Paul had.

How did he do it then? How did he come up with the witness we find in his letters? How did he arrive at his responses to the situations his churches were encountering? What is the nature of the word we have from Paul? How do we understand it as God's word when in fact there is so much of Paul's humanity showing in what he wrote?

We know Paul was human. He contradicted himself, after all. Get married, don't get married (1 Cor. 7:25ff.). There is neither slave nor free, male nor female, Jew nor Greek (Gal. 3:28); but time is short, stay where you are and obey your masters even if in slavery (1 Cor. 7:21; Eph. 6:5; Col. 3:22), and women, hush (1 Cor. 14:34).

We know that Paul was human, that he was intensely emotional. "But even if we or an angel from heaven should proclaim to you a gospel contrary to what we proclaimed to you, let that one be accursed!" Paul wasn't only emotional, he even can come across to some readers as arrogant. "As we have said before, so now I repeat, if anyone proclaims to you a gospel contrary to what you received, let that one be accursed!" (Gal. 1:8, 9).[25]

We know Paul was human — besides being emotional, and perhaps arrogant, he was even forgetful! "You people are saying, 'I belong to Paul, or I belong to Apollos, or I belong to Cephas.' Some of you even go over the top and say, 'I belong to Christ.' Has Christ been divided? Was Paul crucified for you? Or were you baptized in the name of Paul? I thank God that I baptized none of you except Crispus

25. "At several junctures in the history of its interpretation, Paul's letter to the Galatians has been seen as the embarrassing member of the Pauline letter family, the one refusing to be brought into line with the others, and even, in some regards, the one threatening the unity and good-natured camaraderie of the family. . . . In our own century the dominant cause of the letter's being regretted is the obvious fact that, when Paul wrote it, *he was in a state of white-hot anger*" [italics mine]. J. Louis Martyn, *Theological Issues in the Letters of Paul* (Nashville: Abingdon Press, 1997), p. 111.

and Gaius, so that no one can say that you were baptized in my name. Well . . . (scratching his chin and getting lost in memory) . . . I did baptize the household of Stephen . . . (then snapping back to present reality) . . . beyond that I don't know whether I baptized anyone else!" (An interpreted version of 1 Cor. 1:12-16.)

What was it that Paul was doing? How are we to imitate him?

Before moving to a new consideration of what Paul was doing and how we might imitate him for the sake of our preaching, it will be helpful to consider recent homiletical literature as it treats the question of how to preach from Paul. We will find these contributions helpful, especially as they all seek to go beyond merely saying what Paul said. They will also assist us in sharpening the questions we still have to ask and will attempt to answer in this book. We turn now to three contributors to homiletical method as regards preaching from Paul: Daniel Patte, David Buttrick, and Thomas G. Long.

Daniel Patte, *Preaching Paul*

The last thoroughgoing treatment of preaching Paul came in a book by that name by Daniel Patte.[26] Patte flags one of the major concerns I bring to this book, that merely repeating what Paul said does not constitute preaching from Paul:

> Our vocation as preachers or lay people is *not* simply a matter of repeating Paul's teaching, rather it is a matter of expressing the gospel in terms of the experience of those to whom we speak.[27]

Not only is it unfruitful simply to repeat what Paul said, it is also insufficient to repeat an interpretation of Paul from an earlier time and context.

> The first and common temptation is to believe that we preach Paul when we repeat the Reformers' interpretation of Paul. Yet emphasis on Pauline concepts such as 'justification through faith,' 'salvation

---

26. Daniel Patte, *Preaching Paul* (Philadelphia: Fortress Press, 1984).
27. Patte, *Preaching Paul*, p. 9.

by faith alone,' or 'predestination,' was the result of an application of Paul's teaching to a specific situation, namely the sixteenth-century situation in which the Reformers had to confront specific corruptions of the gospel by the Roman Catholic Church of that time. . . . Transmitting the gospel as Paul understood involves applying it constantly to new situations, and expressing it in terms of these new situations, rather than conveying a 'pre-packaged' message. Consequently, *simply repeating* the Reformers' preaching of Paul is, in fact, betraying Paul's gospel.[28]

Patte has his finger on what is perhaps the predominant way Paul is preached today, that of repeating or preaching the Reformers' preaching or interpretation of the Pauline epistles. The Reformers' treatment of the Pauline epistles may have fit their purposes, their historical context, and the needs of the church. We are in a different place and time, however, and a fresh hearing is demanded. We may come to find occasionally — or even often — that the Reformers' hearing of Paul fits our time as well. But we cannot short-circuit the process of listening to the biblical text as found in Paul, by simply running with the fruits of the Reformers' labor.

Through a structural exegesis of Paul's letters, Patte seeks to understand the core dynamics present in Paul's epistles that might instruct us as to the nature of Paul's gospel. If we can understand those core dynamics, perhaps we can reproduce the kind of preaching Paul did. He concludes that three interrelated features characterize Paul's correspondences: they are charismatic, typological, and eschatological.[29]

Paul's gospel was charismatic because it involves the faith conviction of the believer, through which the manifestation of God can be directly experienced. This experience of the believer is not the whole revelation of God, however; it is only a type of the revelation of God possible in Jesus Christ, and therefore it is typological. And the charismatic and typological experiences of the believer are eschatological because they constantly reveal and point to the fulfillment of the promises of God not only in the contemporary situation, but in the future.

28. Patte, *Preaching Paul*, pp. 12, 13.
29. Patte, *Preaching Paul*, p. 16.

The discernment of these three characteristics of Paul's gospel lays the foundation for a series of "theses" Patte proposes as a result of his structural exegesis. At the conclusion of these theses and the notes which support them, Patte lists the following characteristics of genuine and faithful preaching that is founded upon the Pauline epistles. First, our preaching

> needs to proclaim the *kerygma and Paul's teaching as a promise.* . . . Second, our preaching needs to make clear the content of the promise. . . . Third, our preaching needs to be *a preaching of the church to the church.* . . . Fourth, our preaching needs to be *a preaching of the world* (sic!)[30] *to the church.*[31]

Essentially, Patte's characteristics for preaching Paul regard the discernment of the fulfillment of the promises of God in the world as of first order. Communicating the content of the promises of God and pointing to their fulfillment in contemporary life is at the heart of preaching from Paul. The content of the promise may be communicated through the language of first-century Judaism, but the fulfillment of the promises must be reflected by the language and experiences of the local congregation. Consequently, our preaching will involve the church preaching to the church. Persons and events in the church embody the type of faith to which the Scriptures point. It is the preacher's job to notice these persons and their actions, and discern events in the life of the church community in which can be seen the fulfillment of the promises of God. Still further, the preacher must point to the ways in which God has fulfilled God's promises in the world, thereby allowing the world to preach to the church.

In order to do this Patte suggests a hermeneutic is needed to enable discernment of the *fulfillment* of the *promise* of the gospel, and to re-

30. Patte's use of "(sic!)," not mine.

31. Patte, *Preaching Paul,* p. 55. The first three of Patte's characteristics may be more easily understood than his fourth. That our preaching would be a preaching of the world to the church is a call to both repentance and mission. It is seeing "Christ-like manifestations of God in the world in which the Lord precedes us." It is seeing what is truly good in the secular, and of "discovering what are the urgent needs of the world" (p. 56).

late the world and symbols of first-century Judaism to the world and symbols of today. Paul persisted in expressing the promise of the gospel, the kerygma, in the context of Jewish vocabulary. He spoke of the fulfillment of the gospel, however, in terms of his hearers' experience. Therefore, the hermeneutic known as demythologization is not the answer to our need, according to Patte, because the question is not one of translating cultural views and symbolism in order to articulate what is true.[32] If demythologization was to help, it would be because the essence to be communicated would be the truth of the message. Patte claims that the gospel as found in the Pauline epistles, however, points to fulfillment of God's promise in Jesus Christ, not proofs of its truth.

While Patte is clear that demythologization is not the preferred method, he does not develop fully the hermeneutic that will work, nor is he specific about a hermeneutical understanding or method for preachers to follow that is consistent with what we believe about the power of Scripture to speak to contemporary life.

David Buttrick, *Homiletic: Moves and Structures*

While David Buttrick also takes a structural approach to the epistles in the Pauline corpus,[33] he differs from Patte in maintaining that all biblical passages form a "patterned *structure of contemporary understanding* in consciousness."[34] Biblical passages do not convey an idea or a distilled theme, but rather configure a "field of *contemporary* understanding." The passage conveys a patterned field of contemporary understanding in consciousness that then becomes the business of the preacher to convey in the contemporary situation.[35]

---

32. Patte, *Preaching Paul*, pp. 57, 58. Patte defines "demythologizing" as "'translating' given cultural views so as to express those views in a symbolism attuned to the culture of our hearers" (p. 57).

33. David Buttrick, *Homiletic: Moves and Structures* (Philadelphia: Fortress Press, 1987).

34. Buttrick, *Homiletic*, p. 366.

35. In order to come to any degree of understanding of Buttrick's *Homiletic*, one must come to appreciate Buttrick's use of the word "consciousness." The most help-

The Pauline epistles present a peculiar challenge in conveying this patterned field of contemporary understanding in consciousness because they are examples of *non-narrative* biblical literature that require preaching in the reflective mode. The slippery slope to which we are subject when preaching in the reflective mode has two paths down which the preacher may slide. We are tempted to preach either *about* the passage, often filling the sermon with great exegetical detail to explain the meaning of the passage, or we distill a topic from the passage and preach the topic as an eternal truth with contemporary application.

Buttrick rightly points out that neither of these options is a valid way to let the biblical proclamation bring forth a fresh word for today. The challenge, for Buttrick, is "*how* to design sermons in the reflective mode so that sermon structure will relate to the pattern of meaning in our consciousness."[36]

The method for creating such a sermon structure begins with analyzing the structure of thought in the passage. Then the preacher moves to a homiletical analysis of the structure. For each part in the structure of the passage, the preacher searches out the underlying theology, i.e., what are the fundamental theological convictions that seem to support what Paul is saying in the passage? Then the preacher looks for congregation blocks. What will the congregation stumble over, what will be difficult to understand or grasp or what will seem to be

---

ful source for this understanding is David M. Greenhaw's "The Formation of Consciousness," in *Preaching as a Theological Task: World, Gospel, Scripture,* ed. Thomas G. Long and Edward Farley (Louisville: Westminster/John Knox Press, 1996), pp. 1-16. Greenhaw points out that by "consciousness," Buttrick "does not mean a mental awareness, as in 'I am now conscious of the pain in my foot.'" Rather Buttrick seeks to understand preaching phenomenologically, the way in which reality is formed by the phenomenon of lived experience. "The lived experience of grace," for example, "is the experience of grace formed in consciousness" (p. 6). Or, as Thomas G. Long has said, "Buttrick's point of departure from the homiletical pack is his expressed desire to 'describe how sermons happen in consciousness.' In other words, [Buttrick wants to begin] by asking what happens when a preached sermon presses on the keyboard of the listener's mind." Thomas G. Long, review of *Homiletic,* by David Buttrick, *Theology Today* 45 (April 1988): 108, 110-12.

36. Buttrick, *Homiletic,* p. 367.

downright strange and foreign to contemporary ears? And third, the preacher will then gather analogies of understanding from lived experience.

Buttrick's claim is that by moving away from the rationalistic split between exegesis and application, through the homiletical analysis of the passage, we are moving towards forming in our own consciousness a structured field of contemporary meaning analogous to the structured field of meaning in the passage. We will locate fields of experience in our own lives and world that are built not on false analogies (for example, collapsing Paul's use of the term "ambassador" in 2 Corinthians 5:17ff. to mean the same as our understanding of ambassador today), but on a faithful appropriation of the field of "consciousness intending" in the passage.

Buttrick has rightly named the challenge and the potential danger in preaching from non-narrative biblical literature. His approach is helpful insofar as he names the problem of preaching *about* the passage or preaching a *topic yielded* from the passage. He is also right in his attempt to move us away from the pattern of doing historical critical analysis — exegesis — and then moving straight to application with an idea or topic or theme or pearl of wisdom yielded from such an analysis. Buttrick has so insightfully and accurately pinpointed the inherent dangers and pitfalls of preaching Paul, that his methodological solutions merit close study and response.[37]

The underlying principle in Buttrick's system is consciousness. His thorough and consistent use of consciousness represents a theoretical advance in the field and is therefore to be applauded. The problems, however, are spotted when one puts together all the ways in which consciousness is used.

Perhaps the most difficult problem arises from faith consciousness being an exclusively communal event. There is a fundamental flaw at the heart of the system if everything we know about consciousness ap-

37. Parts of this discussion of Buttrick's *Homiletic* are taken from "A Re-Examination of Recent Homiletical Theories in Light of the Hermeneutical Theory of Paul Ricoeur," an unpublished doctoral dissertation submitted to the Faculty of Princeton Theological Seminary by Nancy Lammers Gross, 1992, pp. 60-80.

plies solely to individual consciousness, when preaching is an event which speaks only to group consciousness. Buttrick gives the impression that group consciousness is significantly different from individual consciousness. Group consciousness hears differently, interprets differently, experiences life differently. The move from what we know about individual consciousness to what we know about group consciousness is made uncritically by Buttrick when he claims that faith consciousness is a communal (group) event. That faith consciousness is a communal as well as an individual reality is supported by the apostle Paul and Paul's varied use of the phrase "the body of Christ."[38] That faith consciousness is exclusively a communal event, however, not only contradicts the biblical witness, but also the Reformation and the entire Protestant movement which would claim that ultimately an individual stands alone before God and that each individual has personal access to God.

Once we develop problems with the basic categories of consciousness, it is difficult to hold the rest of the system together. In fact, the role of hermeneutics in Buttrick's system is to encounter the structures of consciousness projected by the text. Discerning the intention of the structure of consciousness of a particular text is the hermeneutical task of the preacher. If we go back to Buttrick's definition of consciousness as a field of awareness, we find that the writer of a biblical text has a "Christian consciousness" that involves being a part of a being-saved community, a community of faith. The biblical writer has an intention regarding the communication of some aspect of life and faith. The particular words used or even the subject matter which is specifically ad-

---

38. Robert Banks makes the point that freedom for Paul consists of three main components: independence, dependence, and interdependence. Persons in Christ are freed for independence "resulting in a personal and life-giving experience of liberty," for dependence "upon Christ, who terminated humanity's enslavement through his death and resurrection," and for interdependence "with others, since liberty leads to service and can only be practically defined in relation to their needs . . . giving liberty a social and cosmic, as well as a personal and theocentric, dimension." Robert J. Banks, *Paul's Idea of Community* (Peabody, MA: Hendrickson Publishers, 1994), p. 25. See also Charles B. Cousar, *The Letters of Paul* (Nashville: Abingdon Press, 1996), pp. 142ff; and C. Norman Kraus, *The Community of the Spirit: How the Church is in the World* (Scottdale, PA: Herald Press, 1993), esp. pp. 31ff.

dressed is not as important as the field of awareness intended by the author.

The goal of the preacher as an interpreter of Scripture is to discern the field of understanding projected by the hermeneutical consciousness intending through the structures of consciousness in a text.

The interpreter of Scripture has a Christian consciousness and is also a part of a being-saved community. The interpreter seeks the field of awareness which is intended by the text, and, indirectly, intended by the author. When the Christian consciousness of the interpreter has grasped the field of awareness, and better yet, the "world of meaning" which is intended by the text, then the hermeneutical task has been done.

The hermeneutical task is complicated, however, by the double consciousness of Christian people. Christian people have not only the consciousness of being a part of a being-saved community, they also have the consciousness of being a part of the world. This double consciousness involves the interaction of the signs and symbols of biblical times with the signs and symbols of our own age. Buttrick's answer to the question of how these signs and symbols relate is that we look in our world for analogies to the signs and symbols to which the biblical text refers.

Add to the complication of the double consciousness of Christian people the special two-way consciousness of the preacher and Buttrick's hermeneutic strains at the seams of credulity. Preachers are like their congregations in every way except that they have been trained for the work of preaching and, in addition to their double consciousness, have a two-way consciousness. Preachers are aware not only of a field of meaning formed by the text, they are at the same time aware of their congregations, particular groups of people formed in given communities of faith.

This puts preachers in a singular middle ground between the being-saved community and the world of the text. Yet Buttrick is confident that the preacher is thoroughly immersed in the being-saved community and has no special Christian experience other than being a part of a being-saved community. The preacher has no special calling or gift for preaching; rather, at most, the preacher has a "kind of fascination with the Mystery whose 'interior' is disclosed in Jesus Christ," and a concern for neighbors. "The sign of a calling would appear to be a disposition toward God and neighbors in faith."[39]

It is hard to conceive how the preacher can possess this two-way consciousness and not be a mediator between people and word. The preacher is to speak of God to the people. How is one to understand a mediator except as one who is called apart? And how is one to be a mediator without processing all that one sees and hears through one's own interpretive framework, one's own passions, understandings, and commitment — or — as Phillips Brooks would say, through one's personality?[40] As I noted before, Paul's humanity, even aspects of his personality, are clearly seen in and through his writings. Paul was writing out of his passionate conviction concerning the Lordship of Jesus Christ and his determination to bring all people, but especially the Gentiles, to faith.

While Buttrick helps to bring the problem of preaching Paul into relief, his solutions rely on what at least seems to me to be a problematic understanding of the nature of the biblical text, the identity and role of the preacher, the nature of the preaching event, and the hermeneutical foundation or method to get us where we need to go.

Thomas G. Long,
Preaching and the Literary Forms of the Bible

The approach Thomas Long takes in *Preaching and the Literary Forms of the Bible* is to look at the way literary genres inform the preaching task.[41] In each chapter Long uses the following questions to give focus to his study:

1. What is the genre of the text?
2. What is the rhetorical function of this genre?

39. Buttrick, *Homiletic,* p. 257.
40. Buttrick, *Homiletic,* p. 459.
41. Thomas G. Long, *Preaching and the Literary Forms of the Bible* (Philadelphia: Fortress Press, 1989).

3. What literary devices does this genre employ to achieve its rhetorical effect?

4. How in particular does the text under consideration, in its own literary setting, embody the characteristics and dynamics described in questions 1-3?

5. How may the sermon, in a new setting, say and do what the text says and does in its setting?

In the chapter on preaching from the epistles, Long examines the nature of the letter and epistle as a literary genre.

Long demonstrates how the genre of the letter or epistle creates a set of expectations on the part of the reader. He shows how Paul used the literary form of the Greek letter as the blueprint for his own epistles. Based on the Greek letter, the New Testament letter is generally made up of a greeting, thanksgiving, body, and closing.

When we receive a letter in the mail, we immediately know this is not a grocery store circular or weekly news magazine. Even subconsciously we have expectations when we recognize the form of a letter in the mail. The opening to the letter further narrows our expectations depending on the nature of the opening. "Dear Sir or Madam," "To Whom It May Concern," "Members of First Presbyterian Church," and "My dearest sweetie," are all ways to begin letters, but depending on the opening, we have very different expectations of what will follow.

Paul typically identified himself as an apostle of Jesus Christ, called by God, and often he flags what might be expected in the letter by the way in which he identifies himself. To the Philippians, "Paul and Timothy, slaves of Jesus Christ;" and to the Galatians, "Paul, an apostle — not from humanity nor through human agency, but through Jesus Christ and God the Father, who raised him from the dead."

After the opening followed the thanksgiving, in which Paul gave thanks for the Christians he was addressing and often for what God had done and promised to do through them. The body of the letter followed, usually with practical and ethical advice. While the bodies of the letters took many forms, Long focuses his attention on the technical rhetorical device known as *chiasmus*.[42] The chiasmus was a way of speaking and thinking, common in the ancient world, in which ideas were arranged in a symmetrical pattern. Sometimes it involved, probably as an aid to memory, the pairing of thoughts in the following manner:

A   First idea
B   Second idea
B′ An idea similar to the second idea
A′ An idea similar to the first idea.

Long goes on to discuss variations on the chiasmic pattern and how the pattern may be employed in preaching. The closing of the letter form included greetings to other saints, final instructions, and often a benediction.

Long accomplishes several things by this contribution to how we might preach from Paul. One is simply to bring into relief how it is that we hear a message differently in the context of a letter than when the same message is brought to us in a different form, such as in person. A second strength is the reminder that the way we begin the letter sends a signal for the tone of the whole letter. A third important observation is the chiasmus form which will train fresh eyes on the epistles for many preachers. The fourth and most significant contribution is the suggestion that sermons might imitate the form of the passage from which the sermon arises.

Long's goal for this proposal is that our sermons might say and do what the Scripture says and does. While not explicitly articulating this concern, one can see how Long's rhetorical method might avoid the pitfalls of preaching the exegesis of the text or explaining a topic or pearl of wisdom distilled from the text.

The question begged when we consider this method, however, concerns the implicit suggestion that the form of the letter will give rise to the faithful word we seek to bring forth from the epistle. There is an inherent coherence between form and content, or between form and

---

42. Long, *Preaching and the Literary Forms*, p. 120.

function,[43] and it makes sense to note how the epistle form accomplishes its intended purpose. This approach does not, however, take into account a more comprehensive hermeneutical approach that will work even if the letter form or the form of the Pauline letter is not what is needed to communicate in the contemporary situation. Put another way, preaching and hearing a sermon is not writing or reading a letter. What is the connection between the form of the letter and the form of the sermon, especially when the form of the letter is often larger than the context of the sermon?

Summary

What is clear from the overview of these three significant contributions to homiletical method in the last fifteen years is that doing what Paul did instead of saying what he said is going in the right direction. All three homileticians spoke of this need in different terms, but all discerned and expressed, implicitly or explicitly, the same problem. Patte's solution was the four characteristics: preaching the kerygma of Paul as promise and making clear the content of the promise; preaching of the church to the church and of the world to the church. Buttrick's solution to the need to do what Paul did was to look for analogous structures of consciousness intending. Long's solution was to look at the literary genre of the letter or epistle and the rhetorical devices employed in the letter in order to say and do in our sermons what the biblical text says and does.

What is missing from these three approaches is a thoroughgoing coherent and comprehensive hermeneutical understanding or method *that is consistent with our theological convictions pertaining to Scripture.* How are we to interpret Paul for preaching? How are we to come to an understanding of how what Paul said has anything to do with what we need to preach today?

---

43. In fact, the connection between form and function is clearly stated in Long's *The Witness of Preaching* (Louisville: Westminster/John Knox Press, 1989), pp. 106ff.

In order to deal with these questions we must next turn to a consideration of what kind of theologian Paul really was. Traditionally Paul has been treated as a systematic theologian. In the next chapter, I will suggest that Paul's work was more that of a practical theologian, reflecting the concerns and foreshadowing the methodologies we consider practical theology today.

CHAPTER TWO

A Paradigm Shift: From System Builder to Conversational Pastor

It was noted in chapter one that following the Reformers' interpretation of Pauline epistles has led to the inclination to treat Paul as though he was a systematic theologian, and his letters, especially Romans, as systematic treatises. Preachers know that Paul's letters were occasional. But we have tended to use the letters as though they were systematic treatises, and we have used the kerygmatic phrases as though simply repeating and explaining them will have the desired effect. If we are not to think of Paul as a systematic theologian, how are we to think of him? What are the alternatives?

In the end, I will propose that we think of Paul as doing the work we attribute today to the practical theologian. But before we get there, we have to take a step back and confront the problem of definition, method, and the delineation of theological disciplines in general.

No less an authority on Paul than C. K. Barrett has observed that whether Paul can be considered a systematic theologian "is a question often answered in the negative."[1] Barrett does suggest, however, that

> beyond the occasionalism of Paul's theology there is a real unity; he reacts to circumstances spontaneously, but he does not react at random; he reacts in accordance with principles, seldom stated as such

1. C. K. Barrett, *Paul: An Introduction to His Thought* (Louisville: Westminster/ John Knox Press, 1994), p. 56.

34

but detectable. . . . To do this is the task of the systematic theologian, who does not need to qualify for the title by writing a large textbook of systematic theology but by his grasp of Christian principles and his ability to think them through and express them in terms of his own environment. It might be said that New Testament theology is the systematic theology of the first century, and this is preeminently true of Pauline theology.[2]

Barrett makes the case for thinking of Paul as a systematic thinker, while wanting not to forget the circumstantial nature of Paul's work and the preaching context in which most of his correspondence took place.

The problem that arises when we start down this path of trying to define the apostle Paul or his work is that the division of theology into discrete disciplines such as systematic, historical, foundational, and practical theology is a modern exercise. We cannot really say the apostle Paul was a systematic theologian or a practical theologian: he was neither. Paul was a Pharisee, a persecutor of Christians who had a life-transforming encounter with the crucified and risen Lord, and then became an apostle. In making the case that the early Christian prophets were the first theologians of the church, Thomas Gillespie makes the point that the message Paul "delivered" was not "taught" to him; rather, Paul "received" his message in the form of tradition (1 Cor. 15:3a). As an apostle, Paul

> received his primordial interpretation of Christ directly from Christ, and is thus at one with all the apostles in the received tradition that 'reflects' the reality attested. It seems appropriate, however, not to designate this primordial interpretation as theology. For theology entails reflection, first as primary reflectivity upon the fate of the reflective language of the kerygma, and then as secondary reflectivity upon the prophetic interpretations of the kerygma.[3]

2. Barrett, *Paul*, p. 56.

3. Thomas W. Gillespie, *The First Theologians: A Study in Early Christian Prophecy* (Grand Rapids: Eerdmans, 1994), p. 241. Gillespie is employing here Robert Funk's three cardinal modes of discourse that may be plotted on a spectrum from that closest to primordial discourse where "language re-flects, without reflecting

The point to be made is that Paul's writings may be understood *not* as theology at all, but as a more primary reflection upon the received tradition, the kerygma, the gospel. The full significance of this will become clear shortly when we challenge the assumptions that Paul was, or was doing the work of, a systematic theologian as we understand that term today.

In working on ancient texts to discern how they might pastorally shape modern readers for a life of "Christian excellence" devoted to God, Ellen Charry observed this problematic situation with modern theological disciplines.

> As I worked through the texts, the divisions of the modern theological curriculum began making less and less sense to me. I could no longer distinguish apologetics from catechesis, or spirituality from ethics or pastoral theology. And I no longer understood systematic or dogmatic theology apart from all of these. In the older texts, evangelism, catechesis, moral exhortation, dogmatic exegesis, pastoral care, and apologetics were all happening at the same time because the authors were speaking to a whole person. *Our neat divisions simply didn't work.* Eventually the distinctions between historical and systematic theology and between theology and biblical studies began to weaken, too. I realized that I was uncovering a norm of theological integrity that had become unintelligible to the modern disciplines.[4]

Charry is challenging us to take off the lenses of modernity that shape the way we read ancient texts, including the Pauline letters. When we view Paul as a systematic theologian, it begs certain fundamental assumptions about what Paul was doing, and then leads us to draw con-

---

upon, the world," to, at the other end, "'secondary reflectivity,'" that which is farthest removed from primordial discourse. The middle point on the spectrum may be called "'primary reflectivity,' in which 'language does not reflect upon language as such, but upon the fate of re-flective language in the face of a concrete but competitive *Lebenswelt*." Funk would characterize the Pauline letter as language in the mode of primary reflectivity, but theology as secondary reflectivity (pp. 238, 239).

4. Ellen Charry, *By the Renewing of Your Minds: The Pastoral Function of Christian Doctrine* (New York: Oxford University Press, 1997), p. viii [italics mine].

clusions about the nature of the Pauline epistles that we would do well to examine more carefully.

Viewing Paul as a systematic theologian leads us inexorably towards saying what Paul said. And while it is true that part of what Paul did was *to say things,* to focus on saying what Paul said leads to preaching by explanation. Understanding better the *function of what Paul was doing* invites us to do the things Paul did. This is not to ignore the content of Paul's writings for the sake of his method, but to suggest that we must not ignore how he got to what he said, or to what end he said it.

The way Paul's writing functioned in his ministry was to form persons for a life of participation in Christ. The function of Paul's writing was to point beyond itself to the new reality, the new age, the new life available in Jesus Christ. Charry says, "the crux of Paul's soteriology is not expiation of sin, but participation in Christ through dying and rising with him."[5] While this is a debatable conclusion from a biblical theological point of view, Charry notes it does lead us to ask the question of what salvation *does* in the lives of the hearers. That question is the point of Charry's study. The manner of the question is coherent with what I think we need to model in our preaching from Paul. That is, we need to do what Paul was doing, bringing the new reality of Christ's Lordship into an engagement with the context in which our hearers live, in order to point the way to new life in Christ.

In some respects it is a violation of the coherent manner in which any ancient author viewed life and wrote, to attach to her or him modern titles or discrete disciplinary definitions. I don't want to perpetuate the problem by now calling Paul a practical theologian instead of a systematic theologian. We have already misconstrued what Paul was doing by thinking of him as a systematic theologian, and there would be manifold problems in simply renaming him with a different modern title. When I propose, therefore, that we view Paul not as a systematic theologian, but rather as a practical theologian, I intend this not to be definitive but descriptive. This is done with the caveat in mind that he

5. Charry, *Renewing*, p. 35.

was not, in fact, a practical theologian. Nevertheless, we need some way to talk about Paul and what he did. We need some kind of model to assist us as we seek to describe what it is we are supposed to do when we imitate him. I will show how looking at Paul as a practical theologian may give us better insight into what Paul was doing when he wrote his epistles, than when we look at him as though he was a systematic theologian.

In order to make the turn from Paul as systematic to practical theologian, we must define what is meant by each term. In a sense I cannot begin to do this discussion justice, for the nature, parameters, and method of theological discussion are significantly in flux today. Furthermore, it is impossible to capture in a chapter that to which others devote whole books. For example, the most popular conception of systematic theologian, that which we have attributed to the apostle Paul, is no longer viable. Systematic theology has changed tremendously in terms of method in the last twenty years. Nevertheless, I will briefly sketch the landscape as I see it and plant a flag where I see how this conversation bears on our understanding of Paul.

A Traditional View of Systematic Theology

Most theological faculties of the nineteenth and twentieth centuries have been organized around what were understood to be the classical theological disciplines: Bible, theology, church history, and practical theology (typically including Christian education, preaching, worship and liturgy, and pastoral theology). Departments in seminaries and divinity schools may have been called by different names, and they may have had subdisciplines, but these four areas have still provided the predominant organizing principle.

Systematic theology as we know it today is a descendent of the post-Reformation movements of confessionalism and scholasticism. Tension and disagreements within Protestantism, and opposition from Lutheran and Roman Catholic churches led to a new focus on method. The organization of ideas along with an emphasis upon a logically coherent and rationally defensible system led to a theological tradition that took general principles to be the starting point, rather than an historical event.[6]

Systematic theology is a reflective task. It draws together many threads of biblical revelation and documented theological reflection through the ages, and shapes doctrines on the foundational themes of theology in an organized or systematic way. Biblical evidence is gathered along with considerations from historical resources and other theologians, and is then weighed and evaluated for its place in the system. The goal of the work of the systematic theologian may still be a text, but the text is not a sermon, per se; it is not preaching or teaching so much as it is framing the core doctrines that inform our faith.[7] It attempts to take disparate testimony and make it coherent.

Systematic theology is a propositional endeavor and not a definitive one because every generation must rediscover and renew a coherent understanding of who God is and who God is calling us to be in Jesus Christ.[8] Every generation must deal with the larger questions and issues raised by its culture. Every generation must put into its own language its experience of God and take into account its own revelatory experience of God when forming its understanding of the system.

Systematic theology is not removed from life; it must take life into consideration. But it is more reflection than it is actively doing ministry as any pastor or congregation would understand ministry; yet systematic theology informs the ministry in which pastors are engaged.

If Paul was a systematic theologian in the traditional, modern understanding of the term, then one would assume that he was in the business of system building. Many view the apostle Paul as a systematic theologian because we have been schooled in a European theological worldview. Robert Jewett makes a compelling case for the way in which the European influence on biblical theology has led us to think

6. Alister E. McGrath, *Christian Theology: An Introduction* (Oxford: Blackwell, 1994), pp. 68, 69.

7. See Paul Scott Wilson, *The Practice of Preaching* (Nashville: Abingdon Press, 1995), p. 192, regarding production of texts being a goal of different aspects of the theological disciplines.

8. Donald W. Musser and Joseph L. Price, eds., *A New Handbook of Christian Theology* (Nashville: Abingdon Press, 1992), pp. 469ff.

of Paul in static, systematic ways. Taking his cues from Stuart Miller's analysis of European character, Jewett observes three qualities of the European intellectual tradition that have heavily influenced Pauline scholarship.[9]

One feature of the European intellectual tradition is the system-building we have already noted. According to Jewett, Europeans love to create a system of thought from which they might work out and argue a consistent perspective. Additionally there is a tendency to be rather defensive about the systems. The style of argument tends to be "eristic," or "fond of wrangling." It is warlike.[10] That many American preachers see Paul as difficult because of his argumentative style was attested by Jewett after traveling around the country noting the lack of preaching from Paul and hearing from preachers why they did not preach from Paul.

A second feature of European life that has characterized the intellectual tradition and has likely influenced Pauline scholarship is the historical reality of hierarchy in social life. Jewett quotes Miller:

> A vague habit of social intolerance, fueled by remembered hierarchy and the fury of revolution both, allows each individual, no matter what his social position, to feel not only that he is right but also that what he thinks in fact represents the right, as embodied in the group.[11]

The egalitarian solidarity of early Christian community might have been somewhat downplayed or disregarded as a result of the age-old European habits of hierarchy and the tendency to impose those hierarchies on other organizational structures. Again, quoting Miller:

> Most fundamentally, the ancient social hierarchy of Europe, surviving intact until very recently and now existing in a debased form, provided men with a continuous visible model for the hierarchy of worth in all things. . . . Even in the kingdoms of the supernatural,

9. Robert Jewett, *Paul: The Apostle to America* (Louisville: Westminster/John Knox Press, 1994), p. 4.
10. Jewett, *Paul*, p. 5.
11. Jewett, *Paul*, p. 7.

there was a hierarchy of saints, angels, and archangels, all leading up to God himself. This sense of an inherent, proper, vertical scheme to everything, with an established aristocracy at the top of the human social order, so un-American, still runs like a current of influence and meaning in the European character.[12]

Miller is right that such a European hierarchy is foreign to the social realities of life in the North American United States, especially insofar as it manifests itself in a caste system, a system into which you are born with little hope of ever escaping. We do, however, experience a form of hierarchical life as it concerns such sociological factors as economic station, gender, age, sexual identity, and race. We do not have a caste system — quite the opposite is our creed. But a hierarchy exists nonetheless. And despite our best egalitarian desires, Paul has held a high place in the ecclesiastical and theological hierarchy of the Christian church, even if it has led many to distrust him or hate him.

A third quality of the European intellectual tradition that Jewett claims has influenced our view of Paul is the propensity to view some historic figures as "great men." The European great man was a glorious man, one of towering virtue and embodying in his intrinsic self and in his intellect superior and aristocratic gifts when compared to the common person.[13] In the European intellectual tradition, according to this argument, Paul was a classic "great man." And there is no doubt that we here in the churches in the USA have inherited, endorsed, and perpetuated this view of Paul, especially throughout our history and through the first three quarters of the twentieth century.

Our tendency to think that Paul was the great thinker who figured out the right theological answers coheres with the European vision of Paul as the "great man." This tendency is also what has alienated so many from the apostle Paul and his writings.[14] The European tendency

12. Jewett, *Paul,* p. 8.
13. Jewett, *Paul,* p. 9.
14. The historic tendency to think of Paul as the great one whose theological precepts are the prescription for life today has led us to think his pronouncements about slaves and women staying in their places were born of a rationally argued, well-thought-out system. They weren't. Those pronouncements were not so much

to see Paul at the top of an apostolic and early church hierarchy is not without compelling evidence. The second half of the book of Acts depicts the travels and travails, the preaching and missionary work of Paul. Towards the end of the Pauline epistles are the Pastoral Epistles, which express a more heavy-handed authoritarianism than we witness in the earlier and more certainly authentic Pauline letters. While in some ways self-effacing, the first letter of Paul to the churches in Corinth apparently goes to great lengths to establish the apostolic authority of Paul. What is wrong, then, with the European vision of Paul as the "great man"?

One thing wrong with seeing Paul as the great one, and therefore his theology as a system to be preached, is that Paul would not have recognized himself as this great one.

> On the basis of traditional depictions of Paul as such a paragon, it was awkward to accommodate Paul's admission that "his bodily presence was weak and his speech contemptible" (2 Cor. 10:10). It was impossible to acknowledge that he sometimes worked under the patronage of others, who in the social context of the Greco-Roman world, were far higher up the social scale than he was, the prime example being Phoebe (Rom. 16:1-2). Although reportedly a Roman citizen, Paul functions as a lower-class handworker, subject to the contempt with which such persons were held in his day, as recent American scholarship has demonstrated.[15]

While Paul was not perhaps a humble man, neither was he narcissistic, arrogant, or interested in self-aggrandizement. He defended his apostleship vigorously in order to defend the truth of the gospel, the good news of Jesus Christ.[16]

---

born of what he thought was the place of slaves and women as they were his passionate concern that nothing impede the survival of the fledgling church and the spreading of the gospel of Jesus Christ. Paul's concern was not keeping slaves and women in their place; it was preparing all for the imminent return of Jesus Christ. Flaunting newfound Christian freedom in social revolution would impede the mission of spreading the good news of Jesus Christ, not help it. The opposite is true today.

15. Jewett, *Paul,* p. 9.

16. J. Christiaan Beker, *Paul the Apostle: The Triumph of God in Life and Thought* (Philadelphia: Fortress Press, 1980), p. 4.

It is easy to see how these characteristics of the European intellectual tradition influenced not only a European view of Paul, but a North American view as well. The fruit of European biblical scholarship is great, and as Beker points out there is no need to argue with the European grasp of Pauline dialectics such as law and gospel, light and darkness, faith and works, the already and not-yet.[17] For all the fruit of European biblical scholarship, however, we err to view Paul as a system builder. It is more accurate to view Paul as a conversational thinker, a dialogical thinker who embraced the pluralism of his age and the different contexts in which his hearers lived.

If Paul were a systematic theologian in our traditional understanding of that term, it is more likely that he would have been concerned with jot and tittle, with adjusting the Jewish law and tradition for Christian thinking. It is more accurate to say that the systematic theology we think is Pauline or inspired by Paul is the Reformers' interpretation of Paul. The Reformers used Romans as a roadmap for their preaching and systematic theological thinking.[18] For the Reformers, however, this preaching was the proclamation of a fresh word brought to bear on *their* contemporary society, as a result of interacting with the Pauline text. We get in trouble when we import the Reformers' preaching in a systematic way, and then consider it our interpretation of Paul.

When Paul penned the words regarding how we all have sinned and fallen short of the glory of God, he was not thinking of these words in bold italics, underlined, in quotation marks, and as a chapter heading. When Paul wrote Romans he did not envision the table of contents of a systematic theology textbook. He was telling the story of salvation, the story of the relationship between God and God's people. Clearly Paul's writing reflects a strategy, a structure, and a coherence. Those rhetorical foundations should not be confused, however, with a modern understanding of systematic theology.

In light of this discussion of what characterizes systematic theology, I find it most helpful to summarize with Daniel Migliore's definition. Theology is

17. Beker, *Paul the Apostle*, p. 12.
18. Thank you to Elouise Renich Fraser for help in thinking about this.

faith asking questions, seeking understanding. It is disciplined yet bold reflection on Christian faith in the God of the gospel. It is willingness to take rational trouble over the mystery of God revealed in Jesus Christ as attested by Scripture. It is inquiry yoked to prayer.[19]

Migliore gathers up the notion of disciplined reflection and introduces the idea of asking questions. It is these two elements which might lead us from what I have characterized as a traditional view of systematic theology to a newer understanding of systematic theology.

A Newer View of Systematic Theology

Nearly twenty years ago the conversation regarding theological method took a leap forward in the publication of ten essays edited by Don S. Browning, entitled *Practical Theology: The Emerging Field in Theology, Church, and World*. What became apparent in these essays is that practical theology cannot be discussed in isolation from theological method in general. This is true in part because as long as systematic theology was about theory and practical theology about practice, the two did not have to relate intrinsically. But as soon as systematic theology begs the "so what?" question and looks at its impact on the practice of ministry, and as soon as practical theology engages praxis, theory-informed practice, then redefining either term has an impact on the other.

In re-envisioning the spectrum of theological disciplines, David Tracy suggested a new definition of theology:

Theology is the discipline that articulates mutually critical correlations between the meaning and truth of an interpretation of the Christian fact and the meaning and truth of an interpretation of the contemporary situation.[20]

19. Daniel L. Migliore, *Faith Seeking Understanding* (Grand Rapids: Eerdmans, 1991), p. 17.

20. David Tracy, "The Foundations of Practical Theology," in *Practical Theology: The Emerging Field in Theology, Church, and World*, ed. Don S. Browning (San Francisco: Harper & Row, 1983), p. 62.

This definition of theology puts dialogue at the heart of the theological task. Discerning the meaning and truth of the Christian fact is an interpretive task in which the truth of the Christian fact is correlated with its meaning. That is, it is one thing to speak the truth, "Jesus is Lord"; it is another matter to come to an understanding of the meaning of the Lordship of Jesus Christ in one's everyday life. Furthermore, discerning the meaning and truth of the reality of the contemporary situation is an interpretive task in which the reality of the contemporary situation is correlated with its meaning. For example, it is one matter to see and take in the horror of two teenagers gunning down their classmates and teacher in Littleton, Colorado. It is another matter to come to an understanding of what that event *means.*

These correlations and interpretations are dialogical in nature. The telos of the dialogue is when the interpretation of the Christian fact is brought into conversation with the reality and interpretation of the contemporary situation.[21] According to Tracy, this is a broad definition for theology as a whole. He then divides theology into three subdisciplines ranging from the relatively abstract to the practical: fundamental theology, systematic theology, and practical theology.[22]

Fundamental theologies abstract from concrete personal experience to focus more on common — or communal — human experience.[23] The questions asked by fundamental theology are broad and general. "Is a religious interpretation of our common human experience meaningful and true? Is a theistic interpretation of religion meaningful and true? Is a Christian interpretation of religious theism meaningful?"[24] The answers to these questions are correlated with interpretations of the Christian fact, demonstrating how even at this broad, abstract level, dialogue is a characteristic of the theological task.

Systematic theologies are the "interpretations of a particular reli-

21. For a helpful discussion of the reluctance of popular media, both print and TV, to interpret the Littleton event theologically, and the imperative for the church to do so, see Thomas W. Gillespie's "Farewell to the Graduates," *Princeton Theological Seminary Bulletin,* Fall issue, 1999.

22. Tracy, "The Foundations of Practical Theology," pp. 62-65.

23. Tracy, "The Foundations of Practical Theology," pp. 66-68.

24. Tracy, "The Foundations of Practical Theology," p. 66.

45

gious tradition in and for a particular situation."[25] The systematic theologian interprets classic texts, symbols, events, and images, and then engages a hermeneutical process in which these classic texts are brought to bear on the particular circumstances of the contemporary scene. The work of the systematic theologian, while particular in focus, is public in nature. Its having particular focus does not lead to privatization; rather, the truth of its findings and claims are open to public testing. The public arena in which systematic theology is done is confirmed by the hermeneutical process where the interpretation is always tested for its validity and truth when it is shared or communicated with another and a new hermeneutical process is set in motion.

The dialogical nature of systematic theology as conceived by Tracy, and its hermeneutical character, are important bridges to practical theology, as we will discover below. The task for practical theology will be to test the vision of systematic theology, and not only to test it, but in testing it and working it out in public ministry, to transform it.

Don Browning takes all of this a step further, saying that all theological disciplines fit under the larger umbrella of fundamental theology. In so doing, he casts systematic theology as that which

> tries to gain as comprehensive a view of the present as possible. It tries to examine the large, encompassing themes of our present practices and the vision latent in them. The systematic character of this movement comes from its effort to investigate general themes of the gospel that respond to the general questions that characterize the situations of the present.[26]

---

25. Tracy, "The Foundations of Practical Theology," pp. 68-72.

26. Don S. Browning, *A Fundamental Practical Theology* (Minneapolis: Fortress Press, 1996), p. 51. Browning is proposing that the overall discipline of Christian theology be called fundamental theology. Under this umbrella, or within this framework, would be the subdisciplines of *descriptive theology*, whose task it is "to describe the contemporary theory-laden practices that give rise to the practical questions that generate all theological reflection"; *historical theology*, whose question is "what do the normative texts that are already part of our effective history *really* imply for our praxis when they are confronted as honestly as possible?"; *systematic theology*, which asks two fundamental questions: what new horizon of meaning is fused

Browning shows how systematic theology moves on a two-way street, from the general themes of the gospel towards our practice of the Christian faith, and from our practice of the Christian faith toward the general themes of the gospel. This furthers the dialogical character of systematic theology introduced by David Tracy. It continues to move us away from the notion that systematic theology moves only from biblical text to human experience.

If Paul was not a systematic theologian in the traditional sense, then perhaps he was a systematic theologian of the type Tracy and Browning are describing. Wasn't Paul, after all, interpreting classic texts and events for a particular situation? Didn't he move both ways on Browning's two-way street? I think the answer is yes. Clearly Paul was an exegete and an interpreter of the Hebrew Scriptures. He also brought to the Hebrew Scriptures and to the "Christ event"[27] the particular circumstances of his house churches and struggling Christian communities.

There are two majors ways, however, in which Paul did not do the work of Browning's systematic theologian. One is that Paul did not try to gain as comprehensive a view of the present as possible. Paul's letters were radically situational. In the process of responding to the issues alive in the churches to which he wrote, Paul did develop themes, a center, a coherent core which expresses his gospel. Nevertheless, he was responding to a specific situation, not generalizing in broad themes to general questions.

The second way in which Paul does not look like Browning or Tracy's systematic theologian has to do with the goal, the telos of

---

when questions from present practices are brought to the central Christian witness, and what reasons can be advanced to support the validity of this new fusion of meaning?; and *strategic practical theology,* which asks at least four basic questions: how do we understand this concrete situation in which we must act, what should be our praxis in this concrete situation, how do we critically defend the norms of our praxis in this situation, and what means, strategies, and rhetorics should we use in this concrete situation? (pp. 47-56).

27. Tracy refers to the work of the theologian as interpreting the "Christian *fact.*" In reference to Paul, I tend to use the phrase "Christ *event*" in order to capture the sense of the new, the immediate, the *eventfulness* for the first-century Christians of Christ's salvific work on the cross.

Paul's work. What kind of text did Paul produce? How did his text function in the church? The fact is that Paul's texts had precisely to do with taking action, with the doing of the interpretation of the classic texts, events, and images. Paul's texts had to do with living out the brief time remaining, according to his apocalyptic expectation, in complete faithfulness to God after the manner of Jesus Christ. The texts that Paul produced did not have to do with a systematic interpretation of the present situation so much as an ethical response to the churches and how to deal with their struggles in light of the Christ event.

I think we will find it more instructive to investigate the nature of practical theology to see if the work of a practical theologian might more closely describe that which Paul was doing. How might we understand his method in our attempt to do what he did, rather than simply saying what he said? We will find a more apt characterization of Paul if we consider a model of practical theology that is coherent with the everyday work of preaching pastors, and with the hermeneutical approach that will be developed in chapter three.

An Overview of Practical Theology

Most practical theologians today credit Friedrich Schleiermacher with setting the stage for the twentieth-century conversation in the methodology of practical theology in his *Brief Outline of the Study of Theology*.[28] While the movement towards discrete theological disciplines was in place long before Schleiermacher, it was Schleiermacher who first advocated that the theological disciplines are several, not one, *and that they are ordered toward the goal of providing for an educated clergy*. According to Don Browning, the consequences of this proposal have been far-reaching, even to the end of this century.

One consequence is the increasing "parochialization or even the clericalization of theology."[29] Theology came to be thought of as prac-

---

28. Friedrich Schleiermacher, *Brief Outline on the Study of Theology*, trans. Terrence N. Tice (Richmond, VA: John Knox Press, 1966). For further reading see Browning, *Practical Theology*, p. 56 n. 1.

29. Browning, *Practical Theology*, p. 26.

tical or applied not because it was applied to thinking and reasoning about the moral life, but it was practical in the sense that it was applied to the responsibilities and tasks of the pastorate. The second consequence of Schleiermacher's proposal is a particular way of relating theory to practice. When theology comes to be about preparing clergy for the tasks of the pastorate, then the study of theology falls into a theory/practice dichotomy. The historical studies of theology — Bible, systematics, and the church — become the theory upon which the practices of ministry are based. Practical theology becomes the study of the practices of ministry. The theory-practice dichotomy engendered by Schleiermacher's *Outline,* though not Schleiermacher's intention, is alive and well today in theological education and is still the organizing principle in many seminary faculties and curricula.

The conversation in practical theology, especially in the last thirty years, deals not only with the problem of the theory-practice dichotomy, but also with how the theological disciplines relate to the world, and to correlative secular disciplines. What are the rules, the techniques for applying the theory learned in the historical disciplines, to the practice of ministry? And how should the discrete curricular disciplines involved in the practice of ministry — Christian education, preaching, and pastoral theology — relate to their correlative secular disciplines such as theories of education, theories of communication and rhetoric and the interpretation of texts, and psychological theories of human development, behavioral psychology and counseling? One might ask, what are the rules of engagement with these various disciplines?[30]

Even more to the point of practical theology is the awareness that despite historical trends, the classical fields of theological study — Bi-

---

30. At Eastern Baptist Theological Seminary, the Christian Ministries Department has analyzed what is offered in the curriculum, what is missing, and what ought to be offered. In the context of these conversations the department has asked whether evangelism, missions, and Christian ethics shouldn't be included. The conversations have been far-ranging enough to lead nearly full circle to what Schleiermacher envisioned, but what never developed: "a single area of theological studies that mediated biblical and historical materials and the issue of the community of faith's self-perpetuation, world-oriented mission, and institutional tasks." Browning, *Practical Theology,* p. 32.

ble, systematics, and the church — are not without a telos that engages the ministry of the church. There is a naturally reflective flow from the historical studies to their implications for today summed up in the question, "so what?," and a need for our inquiries of today to look to the historical disciplines for instructive insight and guidance. Similarly, in the disciplines of the practice of ministry which typically make up practical theology or Christian ministry departments, there is a naturally reflective flow from the techniques of our practice to theorizing how and why we should do things a different way, grounding our work in theory, that is informed both by the historical disciplines of theological studies and secular correlative disciplines. In short, the classical historical disciplines are not only about theory and the practical disciplines are not only about practice.

If practical theology is not only about practice, but theory, then what should be the rightful starting place? Is it our experience in the world? Is it the practice side of the praxis model? Or is the starting place theory, what we believe to be true theologically, or through revelation from God?

Daniel Migliore helps us with this question when he gives a broadstroke sketch of method in systematic theology. Migliore suggests there are three approaches to method in systematic theology.[31] One is the christocentric theology of Karl Barth. Barth's method may be characterized as flowing from the top down, from divine revelation to human experience. The questions of theology are those addressed by God to humanity through the Word of God, and the task of dogmatic theology is to test continually the proclamation of the church against the authoritative divine witness of the Word of God. Most pointedly, the task of systematic or dogmatic theology is to be disciplined not by the questions that arise out of human experience, but instead by the questions the Word of God puts to human existence.

The second method with great contemporary influence is the correlation method devised by Paul Tillich. In the correlation method, existential questions arise from human experience and are then correlated with the Word of God in order to provide answers. Tillich did

---

31. Migliore, *Faith Seeking Understanding,* pp. 14ff.

not think that the normativity of the divine revelation was compromised when anthropological questions initiated the conversation. Nor did he think divine revelation is made normative by the human condition. Tillich saw the task of theology as being more of a conversation between God and humanity than what he characterized as the soliloquy of Barth's method.

The third influential method is the praxis approach of liberation theology. The telos of freedom and justice for which oppressed peoples live and work and fight and breathe is the fuel for this method. It is out of the praxis, or struggle for freedom and justice, that the work of theology is done.

> Beginning with the struggle for change, theology helps to deepen and direct this struggle by recourse to the sources of revelation. Thus "the theology of liberation offers us not so much a new theme for reflection as a *new way* to do theology."[32]

While Barth's questions may be said to come from the top, and Tillich's questions may be said to come from human experience, the questions of the praxis approach of liberation theology truly come from below. They come from oppressed peoples who struggle for justice and freedom, and from those who identify with them.

These three methods, Barth's christocentric, Tillich's correlation, and the praxis approach of liberation theology, set the stage for our discussion of method in practical theology, for one of the most significant questions in practical theology *is precisely* the question of starting point. Do we start with theory, first principles, revelation, what we know to be divinely inspired truth and the dogma or systematics which may be the yield of these questions? Or do we start with practice, human experience, what we know to be true because we have lived it? And as soon as we ask those questions we are confronted with the question of normativity, a question common to both traditional systematic theology and practical theology. When human experience seems to conflict with the divinely inspired Word of God, which one wins?

32. Migliore, *Faith Seeking Understanding*, p. 16, quoting Gustavo Gutiérrez, *A Theology of Liberation* (Maryknoll, NY: Orbis Books, 1973), p. 6.

I am a part of a theological tradition that maintains that the Scripture is the Word of God, and that it is the unique and authoritative witness for life and faith.[33] Properly interpreted, the Word of God both calls and corrects, sustains and chastises, compels us to carry out the mission of Christ in the world and calls us to godliness and piety. We must ask, within this tradition, is there room for questions that are initiated from both above and below? In one sense I would concur that all initiative is from God. God created us, called us, redeemed us, and sets out for us a future in a new heavenly kingdom where there will be no more sorrow and tears, injustice or mayhem. We know we fall short of God's glory because God gave us a law. Without the initiative of God to give us the law we would not know we are lawbreakers.[34] We come to confess Jesus as Lord not because we muster up faithfulness but because of the work of God's Holy Spirit in our lives that brings us to where we can utter the words of faith.[35] In this sense all initiative is from God.

At the same time, and within this broader context of the initiative of God from which all of life and life's questions flow, there is the human experience of initiating questions and engaging in dialogue. We engage in dialogue with one another and with God through the biblical text.[36] We engage in dialogue with the biblical text precisely because God in Christ in the power of the Holy Spirit authorizes such a dialogue by the nature of the textual witness. It is no one of us, nor a group of us, who authorizes this dialogue.

It is the character of this dialogical, conversational thinking that

33. See, e.g., *The Book of Confessions,* Second Helvetic Confession, 5.001; The Westminster Confession of Faith, 6.001 and 6.006; and The Shorter Catechism, 7.002. Also *Book II, The Book of Order,* W.2001.

34. Romans 7:7; John Calvin, *Institutes of the Christian Religion,* ed. John T. McNeill (Philadelphia: The Westminster Press, 1960), II.VII.6.

35. 1 Corinthians 2:9, 10; 2 Corinthians 4:13; Calvin, *Institutes,* III.II.33-35.

36. Browning would characterize all of theology as dialogical in character. He takes David Tracy's definition of practical theology as "the mutual critical correlation of the interpreted theory and praxis of the Christian faith with the interpreted theory and praxis of the contemporary situation," and understands this to be definitive of the fundamental theology, "the most inclusive and central theological enterprise" (*Practical Theology,* p. 47).

correlates so well with the nature of what it was the apostle Paul was doing. The Pauline correspondence engaged many of the activities which we know today as the purview of systematic theology. Paul's goal was not a description of themes, however, nor did he really engage in the business of taking up large gospel themes and applying them to the contemporary situation.

The work of the apostle Paul, as we have evidence in the Acts of the Apostles and in his letters to the churches, was to plant churches, preach, pastor, and respond to the problems his churches were having in their fledgling, newborn existence. Paul's world was diverse and pluralistic, particularly since he understood his ministry to be to the Gentiles. The way Paul did this was to take the "Christian fact," that is, his transformational experience of the crucified and risen Lord, the witness of the early believers, and the Hebrew Scriptures interpreted by the Christ event, and put that into dialogue with his mission as he understood it and the experiences and struggles of his churches. Paul brought to the table both his interpretation of the gospel and his interpretation of the experiences of his churches, and he put them in conversation with each other.

J. Christiaan Beker has made the compelling case that Paul's method was dialogical: a conversation between the coherent center of Paul's thought — which was the Christ event and Paul's apocalyptic interpretation of the Christ event — and the contingent circumstances of the hearers of Paul's letters. Paul's method was the

> hermeneutical interaction between the coherent center of the gospel and its contingency — that is, the manner in which the one gospel of "Christ crucified and risen" in its apocalyptic setting achieves incarnational depth and relevance in every particularity and variety of the human situation. . . .[37]

Beker is saying there is coherent center and contemporary contingency in the expression of the gospel. There is a coherent center to the gospel that can be articulated. There is also the manner in which the gospel reaches into the depths of particular human experience.

37. Beker, *Paul the Apostle*, p. 35.

In responding to Beker's thought Paul Achtemeier has noted that what we have in the Pauline correspondence is not theology so much as theological reflection.

> The basic problem faced by anyone who seeks to find and define Paul's "theology" . . . centers on the fact that we confront in the Pauline letters not so much a theology as a theologian engaged in theological reflection. That reflection, furthermore, is directed not to systematic statements but to the solution of problems that have arisen in different churches facing the varying complexities of attempting to live out the implications of the Christian faith preached to them by Paul and others. Thus, what one confronts in Paul's letters are reflections on how the gospel intersects with the world in which his readers live and how they are to think and act in that world under the rubric of that gospel. That in its turn reflects the fact that what Paul preached, by his own admission, was not a theology but "the gospel" (see, e.g., Rom. 1:16; 1 Cor. 4:15; 15:1; 2 Cor. 11:4; Gal. 2:2; 1 Thess. 2:4).[38]

The gospel is not a ubiquitous, uniform blanket spread over the whole of generic human existence. Rather, the gospel in every time and place mimics the particularity of the incarnation of God in the person of Jesus of Nazareth. The gospel as the in-breaking of God into our lives in Jesus Christ is particular in time and circumstance. This creates the dialogical character of the gospel, and removes us further from a characterization of the gospel as edict or system handed down from on high. We will address Paul's hermeneutical method and the way in which it informs our own hermeneutical method in the next chapter. For right now, it is important to lay claim to this observation that Paul was occasional, contextual, and dialogical.

What we are looking for then is a theological method that is dialogical, the telos of which is a text not systematic in nature, but particular, contextual, time-bound in its historical context in the way God

---

38. Paul J. Achtemeier, "Finding the Way to Paul's Theology: A Response to J. Christiaan Beker," in *Pauline Theology, Vol. 1: Thessalonians, Philippians, Galatians, Philemon,* ed. Jouette Bassler (Minneapolis: Fortress Press, 1991).

entered human time in Jesus. We are looking for a method, the telos of which is a sermon, not an essay or systematic or doctrinal reflection. That is, the story of the Old Testament is that God works in and through history. God chose a particular people, even a despised people, to be a light to the nations. God did not come to earth as a generic human being, but in Jesus of Nazareth, a town from which surely nothing good could come. The theological method we need to support our preaching from Paul is one that honors the specificity of the historical context in which we live, and will lead to a word addressed to particular circumstances.

Our traditional thinking of systematic theological method will not work in conjunction with the apostle Paul because systematics was not his goal; and the generation and explication of timeless topics and themes was not his purpose. If Paul's letters are more systematically reflective than, say, the Gospel narratives, it is because the Gospels tell a story. The Gospels are stories told by those who were with Jesus, or were with those who were with Jesus. Paul's letters bring forth the interpretation of the Gospel story of Jesus, especially as it culminates in Christ's crucifixion and resurrection. But the interpretation is always, even in Romans, brought forth for a particular time and place and circumstance and people, and for a particular purpose. We cannot think of Paul as a systematic theologian in the newer understanding of systematics because Paul's writing points directly to the living out of the gospel, the formation of life as Christ's people, the imperatives and implications of dying and rising with Christ.

If we cannot characterize Paul as a systematic theologian, then I propose we think of him as a practical theologian. Remember the goal is to do what he did, not just say what he said. Therefore we are looking for a methodology that will better enable us to be about the business of bringing the gospel to bear on our context and world. We are looking for a methodological lens that will lead us in the direction of doing what Paul did as exegete and preacher.

I believe the methodology that best approximates what Paul did as exegete and preacher is the revised critical correlation method that was inspired by Paul Tillich, revised by David Tracy, and was significantly influenced by Heidegger and Hans-Georg Gadamer. It is based on the premise that understanding is dialogical and conversational in character, giving rise to a hermeneutical dialogue. Browning character-izes the revised critical correlational approach as that which best con-nects the two poles of theology that tend to split into two camps: "the confessional approach (which sees theology as primarily witnessing to the narrative structure of the faith) and the apologetic approach (which defends the rationality of the faith and tries to increase its plau-sibility to the contemporary secular mind)."[39] If we were to under-stand these two poles from the perspective of Paul's thought, we might say that the Christ event, interpreted through Paul's apocalyptic framework, is the confessional pole, and the particularity of Paul's message, addressed to a particular people in a specific context, is the apologetic pole. Put into Beker's language, the coherence of the gospel is the confessional pole and the contingency of the gospel is the apolo-getic pole.

This is where the work of David Tracy and Don Browning in for-mulating a revised critical correlation method is helpful. According to David Tracy, practical theology takes the interpretation of systematic theology, an interpretation that has already engaged in the process of mutual critical correlation with the particular context, and correlates that interpretation with praxis, or action, or doing. Practical theology goes to ethical action in a particular situation, informed not only by the mutually critical correlation of systematic theology, but with its own mutually critical correlations of the particular situation.[40] The practical theological questions demand that we deal with how to act, how to behave, how to bring about the desired end for which the Christian fact calls, or as Charry would put it, how to live a life of Christian excellence.

A great deal has been said in the homiletical literature about the need for a sermon not merely to say something, but to do something. Fred Craddock led the way in this homiletical development by asking the question, "what is the [biblical] text doing?," and then suggesting that what the sermon does in some way ought to mirror what the bib-

<hr />

39. Browning, *Practical Theology,* p. 44.
40. Tracy, "The Foundations of Practical Theology," pp. 72-82.

lical text does. Thomas Long advocates a *function* for each sermon wherein the preacher is intentional about what the sermon will *do* in the lives of the hearers. Henry Mitchell picks up this theme and insists a sermon must have a *behavioral purpose*. Paul Scott Wilson says that after every sermon, "listeners should be able to discern an answer to the question, 'What is required of us?'"[41] It might be said that this move to what the sermon *does,* its function, behavioral purpose, and answer to the question, "what is required of us?," *is* the move to practical theology. The issue is not so much what the particular function or behavioral purpose of a particular sermon is, since the Spirit of God has a way of working out the purposes of God in spite of us. Instead the issue is that the preacher *has* a function or behavioral purpose in mind. The point is that preachers cannot think they are done with their sermons, or that their sermons are done with them, until the function has been considered. I am suggesting that this is the move to practical theology.

The move from systematic theology to practical theology has been defined above as a move from interpreting the classic texts, events, and images of the Christian fact, to a testing, a living out of the vision of systematic theology. The work of the practical theologian is correlating the vision of systematic theology with an understanding of a particular context that has been achieved through its own mutually critical correlational process. That is, we are not instantaneous knowers of our contemporary contexts, immediately perceiving and simultaneously understanding the meaning of our particular existence. Rather, we come to understand our contemporary context through an interpretive process, a hermeneutical process, correlating our perceptions of the context with previously held understandings and data about the context.

The work of the practical theologian, therefore, is praxis, theory-informed doing. It is ethical action, not simply ethical reflection, in which we work out how to act in a particular situation, how to be-

---

41. A good description of sermonic purpose or function summarizing the homileticians described in this paragraph is found in Wilson, *The Practice of Preaching,* pp. 173 and 186.

have, how our beliefs impact how we live. There is an integration of the reflection upon what we believe with the practical questions of how we live out what we believe. Browning suggests that the questions of strategic practical theology are questions of what do we do in this concrete situation, and how do we think about what we are doing in this concrete situation?[42]

In homiletical language as it pertains to the sermon, this is the question of function, of behavioral purpose, "what are we to do?" The preaching ministry in which the sermons never embody a function leaves a persistent question in the minds of the hearers, "so what?" The preaching ministry that deals only with the "so what?" but grounds the "so what?" on no strong theological and biblical foundation leaves the hearers only with a string of shallow advice.

As a consequence of the two-way nature of this theological activity, the work of practical theology is not only to test out the vision of systematic theology, but in so doing to transform it. That is, our theological vision is transformed when it hits the road. There is an interpretive process, a kind of hermeneutical circle in which the preaching and consequent living out of our theological vision further informs the work of the systematic theologian, which then re-informs the work of the practical theologian, the preacher. In this respect, the work of both theologians is mutually dependent, the lines between the work of the two theologians becomes blurred, and both theologians are engaged in aspects of the work of the other discipline. The piety of the people becomes the telos of our work.

How does this alternative way of thinking about systematic and practical theology have an impact upon our discussion of preaching from the apostle Paul? What is it about the nature of Paul's correspondence that is consistent with the methods of practical theology just described? What is involved in Paul's hermeneutical approach to Hebrew Scripture and the Christ event that can be lifted up by thinking in practical theological terms?

Dialogical reflection, not only between the disciplines of systematic and practical theology, but also within each discrete discipline, co-

42. Browning, *Practical Theology,* pp. 55, 56.

heres well with observations Paul Ricoeur made about the apostle Paul and Paul's method. In an essay entitled, "Preface to Bultmann," Ricoeur discusses the roots of the Christian hermeneutical problem.[43] Ricoeur is referring to more than simply the historical distance between biblical times and now, and to something more specific than the broad claim that understanding is an interpretive process. He is referring to peculiar and inherent problems in the Christian interpretation of Scripture.

Ricoeur discerns three moments in the Christian hermeneutical situation that came to our awareness at different times historically and may be described separately, but in fact are simultaneously present when the biblical scholar, systematic theologian, or preaching pastor approaches the Scriptures. Ricoeur ascribes the first two discernible moments of the hermeneutical problem to the apostle Paul. The hermeneutical problem first arose in dealing with the question, "what is the relation between the two Testaments or between the two Covenants?"[44]

At first there were not two scriptures, but one; not two covenants, but one. There was the Hebrew Scripture, and then there was the Christ event. How does the Christ event relate to the Hebrew Scripture? Ricoeur claims the novelty of the Christ event both fulfills and abolishes Scripture. It effects "a mutation of meaning inside the ancient scripture. The first Christian hermeneutic is this mutation itself."[45] What Ricoeur is describing here is in many ways what preachers recognize when realizing they cannot read the Old Testament without the lens of Christian experience. We cannot avoid being new covenant people when we read the ancient Hebrew Scriptures. The New Testament is, in effect, the spiritual meaning of the Old Testament, claims Ricoeur, and this is the fundamental root of the Christian hermeneutical problem.

Ricoeur credits the apostle Paul with bringing this initial Christian hermeneutic to light because of the way Paul in fact interprets the He-

43. Paul Ricoeur, *Essays on Biblical Interpretation,* ed. Lewis S. Mudge (Philadelphia: Fortress Press, 1980), pp. 49-72.
44. Ricoeur, *Biblical Interpretation,* p. 50.
45. Ricoeur, *Biblical Interpretation,* p. 50.

brew Scriptures, the only Scripture, in his letters. In Galatians Paul speaks of Hagar and Sarah, the two wives of Abraham, and their lineage, and then says, "These things are said allegorically." Ricoeur points out that allegory retains its literary meaning (as a metaphorical analogy), but that the Pauline allegory does so much more. Pauline allegory is "inseparable from the mystery of Christ."[46] The Christ event did not happen out of nowhere. It is inextricably tied to the history of God's relationship with God's people as witnessed in the Old Testament, and the church through the ages has resisted every and any effort to cut the story of Jesus Christ off from the Hebrew Scriptures. The first root of the hermeneutical problem, therefore, is evidenced in the way Jesus Christ, as both exegesis and exegete, transforms our understanding of the Old Testament. This is, in effect, what the risen Lord was doing with the two disciples on the road to Emmaus (Luke 24:27). Surely this was the experience of Paul with the risen Christ on the road to Damascus.

Ricoeur lays the second root of the hermeneutical problem also right at the feet of the apostle Paul. It is Paul who invites us to view the death and resurrection of Jesus Christ through the lens of lived human experience and to view our lived human experience through the death and resurrection of Jesus Christ. Ricoeur puts it this way.

> This idea is that the interpretation of the Book and the interpretation of life *correspond and are mutually adjusted.* Saint Paul creates this second modality of Christian hermeneutics when he invites the hearer of the word to decipher the movement of his own existence in the light of the Passion and Resurrection of Christ. Hence, the death of the old man and the birth of the new creation are understood under the sign of the Cross and the Paschal victory. But their hermeneutic relation has double meaning. Death and resurrection receive a new interpretation through the detour of this exegesis of human existence. The "hermeneutic circle" is already there, between the meaning of Christ and the meaning of existence which mutually decipher each other.[47]

46. Ricoeur, *Biblical Interpretation,* p. 51.
47. Ricoeur, *Biblical Interpretation,* p. 52 [italics mine].

We find here in Ricoeur's observation a hermeneutical coherence with the work of the practical theologian, which is dialogical. This is not simply the old news that the reading, preaching, and hearing of God's word as found in Scripture requires interpretation. While some would still argue that the meaning of Scripture is self-apparent — that it is found on its face, so to speak, that it is plain and means exactly what it says and only what it says — while some would still argue this, it would require of us an infallible, inerrant, and literal view of Scripture. Even with such a view of Scripture, plenty of interpretation is still necessary, since the thought world of the text is other than our own.[48] Pauline letters are still used this way in preaching, even though theoretically the preacher might not agree that this is a valid hermeneutic.

What Ricoeur is getting at is not simply an affirmation of the hermeneutical process. Rather, Ricoeur is saying that imbedded in Scripture itself in "embryonic form"[49] is the hermeneutical situation. One might say that imbedded in Scripture itself in embryonic form is the preaching situation. The essential components that constitute the preaching situation are there imbedded in Scripture: the preacher, the hearers, the context, a hermeneutical process, as well as the word that is proclaimed.

The dialogical, conversational character of practical theology is intrinsic to Scripture itself. The dialogical, conversational character of *preaching* is intrinsic to Scripture itself. When we ask the question, "what was it Paul did?" we *do not* find it to be the case that Paul took timeless truths and *applied* them to the current situation. Rather, Paul was a moderator in the conversation between the Christ event as pointed to in the Hebrew Scriptures and testified to by apostolic witnesses, and the situations in which the hearers of his letters found themselves. It is not the letter form itself, therefore, that is significant as a determinant to sermon structure; rather, it is the organic nature of what Paul was doing in this conversation. Imperative to our preaching from Paul is to enter into this same kind of dialogue.

The third root of the hermeneutical problem discerned by Ricoeur

48. I am indebted to Manfred T. Brauch for this observation.
49. I am indebted to Thomas G. Long for this image.

brings us to the crux of the matter in our thinking about the work and method of systematic and practical theology. The third root of the problem is that even the New Testament itself, a Scripture that we take to be the primary witness and word, "reveals a relation that needs deciphering."[50] While this book has as one of its primary foci the method by which we might bring forth a faithful word from the apostle Paul, the method is not the goal. Neither is the method a "one size fits all" method. At the beginning of this chapter, it was observed that the ancient Christian writers would not have recognized modern divisions of theology. There was a unified vision of theology that Charry argues had as its goal the excellent and faithful living of the Christian life. So also for us, the discussion of method and discrete disciplines must not disguise kerygma, the good news. The third root of the problem is that even Paul's kerygmatic statements, Scripture that we take to be the primary witness and word, are texts that conceal a hermeneutical relation that needs to be exposed.

The situation with which we are faced is that "the Gospel itself has become a text, a letter. As a text, it expresses a difference and a distance, however minimal, from the event that it proclaims."[51] Put simply, Scripture is not the Christ event. Scripture is the witness to the Christ event. The temporal distance between the Christ event and the those who testified to the Christ event in what is now canonical Scripture was so short it appears to us moderns as though there was no distance at all. In fact, Ricoeur claims it took the modern tools of critical analytical method even to discern this distance between the Christ event and the testimony to it. The character of the gospel is that the "kerygma is not first of all the interpretation of a text; it is the announcement of a person."[52]

Thus the somehow accidental distance of a twentieth-century man, situated in another, a scientific and historical culture, reveals an original distance which remained concealed because it was so short; yet it was already constitutive of primitive faith itself. . . . To deci-

---

50. Ricoeur, *Biblical Interpretation*, p. 56.
51. Ricoeur, *Biblical Interpretation*, p. 56.
52. Ricoeur, *Biblical Interpretation*, p. 54.

pher Scripture is to decipher the witness of the apostolic community. We are related to the object of its faith through the confession of its faith. Hence, by understanding its witness, I receive equally, in its witness, what is summons, kerygma, "the good news."[53]

The apostle Paul's words are Scripture, they are authoritative and for us the rule of faith, not because of who the apostle Paul was or what he did, or because he arrived at the right theological answers. His words are Scripture because he faithfully witnessed to the good news of Jesus Christ as he engaged in dialogue and interacted with his churches, and God confirmed this testimony to the hearts of those who have ears to hear and believe. We do well, therefore, not to allow the Pauline corpus itself to be the content of our preaching, but instead, through preaching that emerges from Paul, point to the object of its witness and faith, Jesus Christ.

This brings us back to some of our early questions in contemplating the nature of the theological task for the practical theologian as modeled by the apostle Paul. Where is our starting place, and wherein lies the authority to adjudicate between interpretive options when our experience conflicts with Scripture? Calvin anticipated this question well before the modern division of theology into discrete disciplines.

> But a most pernicious error widely prevails that Scripture has only so much weight as is conceded to it by the consent of the church. As if the eternal and inviolable truth of God depended upon the decision of men! For they mock the Holy Spirit when they ask: Who can convince us that these writings came from God? Who can assure us that Scripture has come down whole and intact even to our very day? Who can persuade us to receive one book in reverence but to exclude another, unless the church prescribe a sure rule for all these matters? What reverence is due Scripture and what books ought to be reckoned within its canon depend, they say, upon the determination of the church. Thus these sacrilegious men, wishing to impose an unbridled tyranny under the cover of the church, do not care with what absurdities they ensnare themselves and others, provided

53. Ricoeur, *Biblical Interpretation*, p. 56.

they can force this one idea upon the simple-minded: that the church has authority in all things.[54]

. . . Let this point therefore stand: that those whom the Holy Spirit has inwardly taught truly rest upon Scripture, and that Scripture indeed is self-authenticated; hence, it is not right to subject it to proof and reasoning.[55]

Calvin reminds us in fairly strenuous language that the church and her preachers dare not decide in the face of modern sensibilities that we know better from our experience who God is and how God chooses to act in the world. The interpretation of Scripture, and most pointedly for this discussion the interpretation of Paul's letters, must constantly be refocused back on the object of the witness of Scripture and the object of the faith of those who penned Scripture. The tendency to isolate Paul, or perhaps some of his letters or some of his statements, as unacceptable in light of modern sophistication is to compromise the unity of the witness of Scripture and thereby to compromise the witness of what would be left after excising Paul. Barth affirms the need for the unity of the witness of Scripture.

Isaiah is not Qoheleth, and Paul is not James. Yet although this is obviously a permanent distinction, it too is relativised by the unity of what is said by all these individuals. When we speak of the biblical witness, we mean this witness as a whole. The distinctions in the content of the witness do not mean a distinction in the witness itself. The Church arose when the witness as a whole was to hand. . . . We cannot separate either the Law and the prophets, or the Gospels and apostolic writings, or the Old and New Testaments as a whole, without at each point emptying and destroying both. If the Church had not from the very first heard this whole, it could not have heard what it did hear. It would not have arisen as the Church. It is only in this unity that the biblical witness is the witness of divine revelation. And remembering this unity, the Church holds fast to this witness.

54. Calvin, *Institutes,* I.VII.1.
55. Calvin, *Institutes,* I.VII.5.

In it it recognises the ruling, divine authority. It busies itself with its exposition. It exists by itself attesting what it finds attested in it.[56]

It is not an option to ask, "should we preach from Paul?" We are required to preach from Paul if we are to hear the unity of the witness to Jesus Christ that established the church in the first place. The witness of Paul to the Lordship of Jesus Christ is not the Christ event itself, but it is constitutive to the witness of Christ that must be proclaimed again and again for the church to be the church. The witness of Paul must be tested in the context of the entire biblical witness, and the balance of the biblical witness must be tested in the context of Paul's epistles. It is not Paul, and then the rest of the biblical witness. It is the entire biblical witness to which we must attend, including no less than a full hearing for Paul.

The proclamation that comes forth from the Pauline epistles must be fresh in every age. It must converse with the contemporary context and say that which must be said to the contemporary manifestations of the "elemental spirits of the universe."[57]

> *Proclamation must ever and again become proclamation. . . . And because the event of real proclamation is the function of the Church's life which governs all others, we have to say that in this event the Church itself must ever and again become the Church.*[58]

The witness that emerges from Paul cannot be conditioned by our dogmatic or systematic sense of what Paul means. Rather, our dogmatics and systematics are made ever new by the faithful proclamation from Paul.

> Church proclamation is the raw material of dogmatics. But it would be a fatal confusion to try to reverse this and say that dogmatics is the raw material of proclamation.
>
> It is a familiar and perhaps unavoidable beginner's mistake of

56. Karl Barth, *Church Dogmatics*, ed. Bromiley and Torrance (Edinburgh: T. & T. Clark, 1956), 1.2:482.
57. See sermon in chapter five, "Hidden Lives."
58. Barth, *Church Dogmatics*, 1.1:88 [italics mine].

students and assistants, when preaching, to think that they can and should confidently take the content of their preaching from their treasured college notebooks and textbooks of dogmatics. On the other hand, older preachers are usually far too confident in removing themselves from the jurisdiction of this critical authority.

One cannot and should not expect to hear the content of proclamation from dogmatics. *This content must be found each time in the middle space between the particular text in the context of the whole Bible and the particular situation of the changing moment.*[59]

Karl Barth, the one whose theology is most popularly understood as coming from above, here affirms the centrality of the dialogue between the biblical text in the context of the unity of biblical witness, and the ever-changing contemporary context as the source of our dogmatic theology.[60] Barth said it most clearly: preaching is the raw material of systematic theology; systematic theology is not the raw material of preaching.

While many might affirm in principle this dialogue between text and context as constitutive of preaching, we deviate from this principle in two primary ways in our preaching. One tendency is to be confirmed in our dogmatics or systematics before we approach Scripture. We already know what it means because we already know what Paul thinks. Paul has defined our system, and therefore we go to Paul to prove and illustrate what we already know we want to say. Essentially, we find in Paul what we expect to find. That is one way we commit the error of making our systematics the raw material of our preaching.

The other way we deviate from the principle of the dialogue between text and context, making our systematics the raw material of our preaching, is when we objectify or fossilize Paul's letters. Many who fall into this objectification of Paul's letters cease to preach from Paul because they find so abhorrent that which they have objectified. For some, the objectification of Paul's writing crashes into our experience in the world with such discontinuity, and for others, even vio-

59. Barth, *Church Dogmatics,* 1.2:79 [italics mine].
60. I am indebted to Daniel Migliore for highlighting this aspect of Barth's approach.

lence, that Paul gets put aside as a matter of personal and spiritual survival.

Many others who err in the direction of fossilizing or objectifying Paul's letters *do* preach from Paul and do so because of their high view of the authority of Scripture. They grasp wholesale everything Paul wrote, on its face, and end up merely saying what Paul said, often from the point of view of an isolated and detached authoritarianism. The danger here is a distortion of what Long calls the "herald" image of the preacher. The herald is one who has a message from the king.[61] The herald does not "interpret" the message of the king. The herald simply delivers it. Barth himself gave rise to this image: "Proclamation is human speech in and by which God Himself speaks like a king through the mouth of his herald, and which is meant to be heard and accepted as speech in and by which God Himself speaks."[62] In his preaching, however, Barth was contextual and attentive to the life situation of his hearers.[63]

Barth claimed that no matter how many times preachers disappoint them, people come to church at the ringing of the bell with an air of expectancy that something momentous was about to happen. People come not only expecting something to happen in church, but hoping to hear the answer to the question, "Is it true?"

> Is it true, this sense of a unity in diversity, of a stationary pole amid changing appearances, of a righteousness not somewhere behind the stars but within the vents which are our present life, of a heaven above the earth — not only *above* the earth, that is to say, but above the *earth?* Is it true, this talk of a loving and good God, who is more than one of the friendly idols whose rise is so easy to account for, and whose dominion is so brief? What the people want to find out and thoroughly understand is, *Is it true?*[64]

---

61. Long, *The Witness of Preaching* (Louisville: Westminster/John Knox Press, 1989), pp. 24-30.

62. Barth, *Dogmatics*, 1.1:52.

63. Long, *The Witness of Preaching*, p. 30.

64. Karl Barth, *The Word of God and the Word of Man*, trans. Douglas Horton (Gloucester, MA: Peter Smith, 1978), p. 108.

When people come to church asking, "Is it true?," they are asking for more than to have their experience confirmed. They want to know if there is a God beyond the idols of their own making. They want preachers "to understand them better than they understand themselves, and to take them more seriously than they take themselves."[65] The seriously-minded preacher cannot take the easy way out and merely mimic the words of Paul, scratching the surface of life by applying them glibly to the life and death struggles of people in the pews.

The gospel of Jesus Christ as attested in Paul's epistles will withstand any question brought by the human situation; it will plumb the depths of human experience, for God has already gone there. The people come because no matter how poorly anyone of us might do Sunday by Sunday, the Holy Spirit continues to create in our hearts an expectancy that only in sitting before the word of God, the whole counsel of God, will we find the answer to the question, "Is it true?"

> The event toward which this expectancy is directed . . . is Christian preaching. . . . As the minister of the people who come or do not come to church on Sunday, [the preacher] must be the first to give them the *answer;* and as the minister of the Bible [the preacher] must be the first to be prepared to submit to God's *questions* by asking the question about God, without which God's answer cannot be given. If [the preacher] answers the *people's question* but answers it as [one] who has . . . been *questioned by God,* then [the preacher] speaks — the word of God; and this is what the people seek. . . . For being truly questioned by God and truly questioning about God, [the preacher] will know God's answer and so be able to give it to the people, who with *their* question really want *God's* answer, even when they do not realize it.[66]

The question "Is it true?" is answered by God's "Yes"! in Jesus Christ (2 Cor. 1:19, 20). The preacher submits herself again and again to the Scripture, to the questioning by God, and to ask questions of God, on

65. Barth, *Word of God,* p. 109.
66. Barth, *Word of God,* pp. 122, 123.

behalf of a people who have nowhere else to turn for a true word. Listening for this word is both more difficult and more frightening than being even mildly influenced by the "elemental spirits of the universe," or by fossilizing and objectifying Paul's words either to reject or woodenly mimic them. But to this high purpose we are called.

To recapitulate, one of the roots of the hermeneutical problem is that the gospel is not first of all the interpretation of a text, but kerygma, good news, the announcement of a person. We have come to think of Paul's writings as the gospel when, in fact, his writings are the interpretation of the announcement of a person. This revelation both frees us and binds us theologically. We are free to be forward-looking with the biblical text in order to see that to which the text is pointing. We are free to hear the announcement, to hear the kerygma, the goods news. At the same time we are bound. We are bound to the one whom the text announces, Jesus Christ, as he is attested in the unity of the biblical witness.

Summary

The goal of this chapter has been to describe a theological methodology for preaching from Paul that will free us from a traditional systematic in which we are pressed merely to say what Paul said. The conversational nature of the practical theology that goes beyond general themes to the living out of our Christian faith in particular times and places and circumstances, is a more faithful understanding of what Paul was doing.

I cannot help but wonder if the weakened state the church finds itself in today cannot be attributed in part to any or all, or some combination, of the following:

a. our failure to proclaim the unity of the witness of Scripture, including the Pauline epistles;

b. our failure to proclaim the object of the apostolic faith without embarrassment: the crucified and risen Lord;

c. our failure to set right the relationship between dogmatics and proclamation, putting the systematic cart before the proclamation horse;

d. our failure to put into conversation the apostolic witness as we have it from the apostle Paul and the contemporary context in which we live.

The positive way to state these essential factors in thinking about preaching from Paul, the correction to these failures, is to

a. proclaim the unity of the witness of Scripture, including the Pauline epistles;

b. proclaim the crucified and risen Lord, the object of apostolic faith, without embarrassment, even if we are occasionally embarrassed by Paul's thoroughgoing entrenchment in the sociocultural realities of first-century Palestine; proclaim the cross of Christ with a passionate determination not to flatten the scandal of the cross in the face of modern sensibilities;

c. rely on Scripture as the raw material of the church's proclamation, not on our systematic theological thinking derived from Scripture;

d. be a moderator in the conversation between Paul's witness to his house churches and the infant Christian community, and the particular context that makes up the world of a specific group of hearers, the congregation.

The goal of our preaching must mirror Paul's: "to bring about the obedience of faith among all the Gentiles for the sake of Jesus' name" (Rom. 1:5); and to work that we may stand blameless before God on the day of our Lord Jesus Christ (1 Cor. 1:8). In the next chapter, I will propose a hermeneutical approach that may enable such faithful preaching.

CHAPTER THREE

A *Paradigm Shift:*
From Bridge to Swing

In chapter one we found that there have been some important advances made in the last fifteen years in how we might preach from the Pauline epistles. It appears the most vexing problem is that there is not a clear method for interpreting what to preach from Paul that would then suggest to us how we go about preaching it. In chapter two we discovered more about the apostle Paul, how he could be better described as a practical theologian than a systematic theologian, and we considered how models of practical theology are important models for the consideration of preachers and pastors. We are now prepared to rethink our hermeneutical approach to the Pauline epistles for preaching.

Stated even more clearly, we know that exegetically explaining a Pauline passage, in and of itself, is not necessarily the most faithful way to preach Paul. We know that distilling a Pauline passage into a kernel of truth or a topic for the day may lead to distortion. We know that Paul was not a systematician, that his epistles were not a syllabus for a systematic theology course, and that our theology as derived from — or over against — Paul cannot be the raw material of our preaching. How then do we go about preaching from Paul? What kind of hermeneutical process will assist us in doing this task more faithfully, avoiding the pitfalls mentioned in chapter one and the errors with method described in chapter two?

In this chapter I will discuss a hermeneutical approach for preaching from Paul. The description of the method itself will come in chapter four. Here we must examine an approach that will enable us to avoid the common errors earlier described, and chart a path where we might do what Paul did.

In order to get at this approach, we must first uncover a deeper issue hidden beneath this question of hermeneutical approach. This deeper issue goes to the heart of how we interpret biblical texts for preaching, even the relationship between homiletics, the business of preaching, and hermeneutics, the business of interpretation.[1]

The word "hermeneutics" is widely used today, and has been used broadly in the past. The term has had a long career as the general science of interpretation in both theology and the human sciences, but its meaning has gradually changed over the years. Where once hermeneutics referred to linguistic rules for the interpretation of an ancient text, it has been broadened today to stand, in many cases, for an entire phenomenology of knowledge.

To further complicate things, the form of the word "hermeneutics" has been stylized to refer to a particular approach, as in the "New Hermeneutic," suggesting a radical departure from what was presumably the "old" hermeneutic. The "New Hermeneutic" refers to the double awareness that the ancient text is conditioned by its historicity and that its modern interpreter stands in historical context as well.[2] The consequence of this double awareness is that the text becomes a subject which interprets the modern reader, even as the modern reader interprets the text.

Beyond this fundamental distinction between old and new hermeneutics, the term "hermeneutics" can refer to theories of biblical exegesis, rules of philology, cultural interpretation, and juridical applications.[3]

1. Portions of this chapter and some of the core ideas therein were first presented in the unpublished dissertation, "A Re-examination of Recent Homiletical Theories in Light of the Hermeneutical Theory of Paul Ricoeur," especially pp. 1-5, 13-19, and 114-69.

2. See Anthony C. Thiselton, *The Two Horizons* (Grand Rapids: Eerdmans, 1980), pp. 10ff., for a concise discussion of the development of the term "hermeneutics."

3. A helpful discussion of modern definitions of "hermeneutics" can be found in

For our purposes, when I use the term "hermeneutics," I mean the interpretation of texts in which there is both an overall description of the process of coming to understanding and a procedural method for coming to understanding.

The problem to which I allude above, the deeper issue hidden beneath the questions of hermeneutical approach, is a problem that exists in modern homiletics, and which is brought into distinct relief through much of our preaching from the Pauline epistles.

The problem is a chasm that exists between the exegetical work we do with the biblical text, and the homiletical work of sermon preparation.

The problem comes to our awareness as a result of the revolution in hermeneutics which has taken place in the last fifty years to produce the "New Hermeneutic."

The problem is rooted in the adoption by modern homiletics of the old, Romanticist hermeneutics of Schleiermacher and Dilthey — a hermeneutic that maintains a dichotomy between the concepts of "understanding" and "explanation." In Romanticist hermeneutics, understanding and explanation were seen as two distinct ways of knowing, two modes of intelligibility.[4] This led to a two-step hermeneutical process.

Gathering meaning from a text was the first step in the process and was known as "understanding." Understanding has to do with grasping the meaning another intended through a written text. This was generally conducted under the rules of biblical exegesis. All seminary-trained preachers are aware, sometimes painfully so, of this part of sermon preparation. So extensive are our various methods of histor-

---

Richard E. Palmer, *Hermeneutics* (Evanston: Northwestern University Press, 1969), pp. 3-45.

4. See Palmer, *Hermeneutics,* for a discussion of the hermeneutics of Schleiermacher (pp. 84ff.) and Dilthey (pp. 98ff.), and the role they played in the development of modern hermeneutics.

ical-critical analysis that many preachers despair of ever fully exploring a biblical text. Time-pressed preaching pastors often feel they have cheated their congregations and compromised their own standards when they do not adequately exegete a text, and many are motivated by the fear that if they do not do their homework with a text, they will commit the grievous and hated sin of eisigesis.

Eisigesis is usually understood as putting one's own meaning into the text, rather than getting the meaning out of the text through responsible use of exegetical tools. Even this tried and true characterization falls prey to old hermeneutical assumptions, however. Whether thinking exegetically and "getting the meaning out of the text," or eisigetically and "putting one's own meaning into the text," one has not come to conclusions about the text through a conversational process with the text. Whether we err on the side of exegesis or eisigesis, there is still a one-way conversation going on, not the dialogue described in chapter two. In any event, in the Romanticist hermeneutical model, once one has found the meaning of the text, an "understanding," the preacher is ready for the second step, "explanation."

Explanation is describing, explaining, translating, or illustrating the meaning of the text for today's world. A survey of homiletical literature leading up to twenty years ago will show that explanation became the business of modern homiletics. The homiletical textbooks of the 50s, 60s, and 70s show the extent to which the focus in preaching method was on how best to explain a meaning found or distilled in the text to a modern congregation through various schemes of explanation.[5]

In many respects the narrative movement in preaching was a response to the wooden nature of this two-step process — understanding and explanation. There was an attempt to find a more lively way to hear biblical texts in preaching and to wed the biblical story with our story, to see how our story fit into the biblical story. We will see later in this chapter, however, that while narrative approaches paid more at-

---

5. See, for example, George E. Sweazey, *Preaching the Good News* (Englewood Cliffs, NJ: Prentice-Hall, 1976); and John Killinger, *Fundamentals of Preaching* (Philadelphia: Fortress Press, 1985).

tention to homiletical form, they did not deal at a fundamental level with this dichotomous split between understanding and explanation.

The result of this split between understanding and explanation, this two-step process in which understanding or exegesis is divorced from explanation or sermon creation, is that homiletics has become, in its theoretical base, estranged from the text that gives it life, the biblical witness. There is a chasm, a gulf between exegesis (understanding) and sermon creation (explanation).

In homiletical literature the dichotomous split between under-standing and explanation creates considerable confusion or wrongheadedness at two levels: (1) the unexamined assumption that hermeneutics is a step in the homiletical process; and (2) the lack of method for moving from text to sermon once we do straighten out the relationship between hermeneutics and homiletics.

Hermeneutics and Homiletics

First Level of Confusion — The Chasm

The first level of confusion is the unexamined assumption that the hermeneutical process is only a step in the homiletical process. By "hermeneutical process" I mean the process by which a text finds expression in a sermon. In other words, the hermeneutical process would be the way in which the preacher presides over the text to sermon process. By "homiletical process" I mean the traditional process of sermon preparation where an insight that has been gleaned from Scripture is then crafted into a sermon. The dichotomous split between understanding and explanation that persists in homiletical literature today leads to hermeneutics being the step of interpretive leap within the homiletical process.

This hermeneutical step, or interpretive leap, has often been characterized as a chasm, a gap or a breach which has to be crossed. The metaphor is that the preacher must build a bridge or cross a bridge, leaving the side of the congregation and contemporary life and crossing over to the side of the text, there investigating the text. Once a meaning or understanding has been gleaned from the text, the preacher must cross back over the chasm to the congregation where a sermon can be developed that will explain the meaning found in the text. The bridge, the crossing over, is understood to be the hermeneutical step. The leap from exegesis to sermon creation is the interpretive leap where the preacher figures out what this text has to do with contemporary life.

The preacher has to find some way to get from understanding to explanation. There is a chasm between the two modes of thinking, the two ways of grasping the meaning of the text. Every preacher who has ever exegeted a text and come up with a major theme to preach, and then has wandered around for days wondering how to "get it across" to the congregation, knows the experience homileticians describe as a chasm or gulf to be crossed. The leap from understanding to explanation has traditionally been the hermeneutical step. We have taken the meaning from the ancient text and looked for ways to interpret it to modern ears. The process is one of three steps:

Understanding — Hermeneutical Leap — Explanation
or
Exegesis — Hermeneutical Leap — Sermon Creation

In effect, the hermeneutical step is one step within the homiletical process. Another way to express this first level of confusion is to say that homiletical literature reflects the unexamined assumption that hermeneutics is a figure against the ground of homiletics.[6] Traditionally homiletics has been the ground, the field of vision, with hermeneutics being only a piece or a figure against the ground. Homiletics is the field which governs the use of hermeneutics in the practice of contemporary

6. By "figure-ground" I am thinking of Michael Polanyi's usage referring to field of vision and a particular against the field. See Michael Polanyi, *The Tacit Dimension* (Gloucester, MA: Peter Smith, 1983), especially ch. 1.

preaching. In fact, homiletics is unwittingly governed by the Romanticist hermeneutics described above. Homiletics has become the business of "explanation." Yet within the process of explanation the step named hermeneutics is inserted.[7]

Edward Farley has named this condition in homiletics the "bridge paradigm" and claims it is the single largest barrier to biblical preaching today. The bridge paradigm is problematic because it invites preachers to preach the content of *passages* of the Bible instead of the gospel of Jesus Christ. Preaching a passage of the Bible is precisely *not* preaching the gospel, according to Farley, because the gospel is the whole story, the collection of themes, events, personal stories, poetry, and law. The logical extension of this thinking is that a kind of biblical fundamentalism is unavoidable when preaching a distinct passage or pericope of Scripture. Those commonly thought of as fundamentalists, that is, those who take the words of Scripture to be literally true and inerrant, bear great resemblance to the preacher who operates within the bridge paradigm of preaching, as Farley's thinking goes. While the bridge preacher may consider the historical, contextual origins of Scripture and may avoid proof-texting by considering the broader context of a passage, a new kind of fundamentalism has been introduced by this bridge preacher, according to Farley, because the new contextual unit is taken to be authoritative in some isolation from the rest of Scripture.[8]

7. See, for example, Paul Scott Wilson, *The Practice of Preaching* (Nashville: Abingdon Press, 1995), p. 124.

8. Edward Farley, "Preaching the Bible and Gospel," *Theology Today* 51 (April 1994): 93-95. Farley's critique of the traditional preaching model in which the Bible is carved up into passages is well taken. Many who preach from the Revised Common Lectionary experience this often because of the frequency with which the lectionary prescribes short passages of Scripture. The preacher is in charge of deciding upon the beginning and ending of a Scripture text, however, even when preaching from the lectionary; and furthermore, it is the preacher's responsibility to place each passage of Scripture, long or short, into not only its immediate context, but the context of the biblical witness as well. (On April 6, 1999, Nora Tubbs Tisdale hosted Eugene Lowry, her Homiletical Theory Ph.D. Seminar, and several other interested parties, where we discussed the work of David Buttrick. I am indebted here to those conversations, and particularly to Lowry's references to Farley's work.)

Beyond Farley's critique, there are several problems with this two-step process with the leap or bridge crossing in the middle. First, the root of these problems is that traditional homiletics has become the second part of the Romanticist hermeneutical dichotomy. Once a "meaning" is derived from the process of understanding, it is carried over to the new mode: explanation. The homiletical method then takes over, showing how best to explain the meaning. The homiletic, in fact, becomes independent of the act of interpretation. It falls into the explanation mode of intelligibility and there is nothing within the homiletical system itself which can bridge the chasm between the two modes of intelligibility.

Second, homiletical theories that are built on the dichotomous split between understanding and explanation give rise to preaching that suffers from objectification, precisely the kind of objectification we tried to overcome in chapter two. The homiletic becomes quantifiable and objectifiable, rather than eventful. If the eventfulness of the encounter with the text takes place in the understanding mode, the homiletical method, and the preaching itself, falls into a strictly cognitive or explanatory mode. There is nothing within the homiletical system to bridge together these two essential parts of the preaching task.

Third, when homiletical theory is reduced to the explanation mode of intelligibility, it tends to become a game of rearranging the interchangeable pieces of a puzzle. One method may place the emphasis upon the preacher, another method may place the emphasis upon the hearer, or context, or the content of the message. There is, however, no central governing factor to provide the coherence for the constitutive factors of preaching. Something larger than any one of these factors is needed to unify the system.

Fourth, due to this dichotomous split between understanding and explanation, there is no central factor to govern the critical approaches to biblical study, such as genre identification, structuralism, or historical-critical methods. These all become external to the homiletical system itself.

This difficulty with the critical tools of biblical study points to a fifth, and still more serious, problem: namely, the relation between Scripture and homiletical theory. The faulty view of hermeneutics, upon which traditional and contemporary homiletics is based, obscures a faulty view of Scripture. The implicit assumption is that a biblical text will yield some "kernel" of meaning whose destiny is then to be objectively explained. It implies that in our study of the biblical text we are engaged in hunting treasure or harvesting oysters for pearls. The logic here is, if we can just clear away the sand to expose the pearl of meaning, then we can explain the meaning in the sermon.[9]

This view of Scripture errs on many levels. It turns the biblical witness into an objectified, exteriorized collection of truth statements or true ideas. This is where I agree with Farley's analysis of the problem with preaching from the bridge paradigm. The question that remains is how the discrete passage of Scripture points to the larger message of the gospel. When we take Scripture to be a collection of truth statements or true ideas, it puts the interpreter in complete charge of the process, from searching for the true idea to giving language to the idea, to explaining the idea. It overlooks the significance of the various literary forms of the Bible, namely, that these literary forms embody meaning intrinsic to them, rather than serving merely as clever vehicles for conveying objective meaning extrinsic to their forms. Finally, this view of Scripture ignores the complexities and nuanced nature of Scripture and the possibility that different people will hear the witness of the Scripture differently. We are left instead with the impression that Scripture is one-dimensional and that there will be a uniform way of hearing its witness.[10]

---

9. This is essentially Farley's objection, the content-of-the-passage orientation to bridge paradigm preaching. He contends that the preacher who operates in this mode will tend to preach not the gospel to which the passage points, but the content of the passage. I think many preachers experience a cognitive dissonance between the methods they have been taught that lead to bridge paradigm preaching and their own intuition that would lead to preaching the gospel. As I will indicate in chapter four, so much of what preaching classes teach is built on the foundation of biblical and exegesis classes, that it is difficult for preachers to overcome the early training of thinking that exegesis yields the meaning of the passage which will lead to the content of the sermon.

10. The question begged is whether there aren't some passages in Scripture that indeed contain "truths," or truth statements. Are there not places in Scripture where cognitive content can be grasped and its meaning does not depend upon form? The

Sixth, because current homiletical theories start with preaching itself, they tend to move backward into theory and forward into method, creating a theory/method dichotomy which we saw in chapter two did not exist in biblical times or in the early church, and which those who think about practical theology are trying to overcome. Once again, what is missing is a compelling and internal coherence.

Essentially the bridge paradigm in preaching leads to homiletics that is all about method, but is cut off from both Scripture that gives rise to preaching in the first place, and then theological reflection upon the nature of the preaching task.

Many may object to the above characterization of the problems we suffer when the chasm between understanding and explanation organizes our homiletical methods. I would suggest, however, that every time a preacher says, "the fourth and final thing this passage tells us is . . ." or when Sunday after Sunday the Scripture always tells us three things, the Scripture has been objectified, and the sermon itself, the preaching event, has been cut off from the source that gave it life.

All of these problems lead to the reality that many preachers intuitively find another way of proceeding besides the homiletical systems that are built on the two-step model. Preachers who intuitively preach biblically do not find themselves strictly on one side of the bridge or the other. They find themselves in the process of sermon construction even as they are investigating the text. They hear sermons or preaching moments even as they are initially listening to the text. What is happening is that the text is straining forward to be heard again, the text is pointing to the gospel even as the preacher is muddling through a mechanical process in search of the morning message.

Preachers who have been trained to do exegesis first and then

---

frequency with which we quote and stand upon the promise from Ephesians 2:8, "For by grace you have been saved by faith," or Galatians 3:28, ". . . for all of you are one in Christ Jesus," would seem to indicate such a self-apparent cognitive truth. While these passages are true and meaningful to those of us who believe, they are filled with meaning by the witness of the Holy Spirit in our hearts and our experience of God in the world. Both the witness of the Spirit and our experience of God in the world can happen apart from preaching. But God chose the folly of our preaching to save those who believe, and no matter how we cut it, preaching is an interpretive act.

carry the discovered meaning over to sermon construction often feel guilty that the cart of the sermon seems to be getting ahead of the exegesis horse. I have had seasoned preachers confess to me with great embarrassment that they made connections to life images and stories even before they had done much critical work with the text, that the sermon began to form in their minds prematurely, before they had done their exegesis of the text. If they let any of that premature sermon become a part of the final baby, they somehow felt they had cheated the process and not truly listened to the text.

It may in fact be true that sometimes these preachers did not listen to the text or that they did not let the text correct a previously-held view of the world or previously-construed notion of the meaning of the text. It may also be true, however, that the preacher heard a valid and needed word of proclamation early in the process and that the critical work done with the text simply supported this voice and validated its meaning. It may be the case that as the preacher sat before the text and listened and conversed with the text, the world of the gospel of Jesus Christ was being opened, pointed to, heard over and above the din of our exegetical and homiletical methods.

Attempts to Overcome the Chasm

Many homileticians have recognized or sensed the problem of the split between understanding and explanation, or exegesis and sermon construction leading to the bridge paradigm, even if they haven't named it or fully disclosed the source of the problem.

This gap or chasm is in part what Fred Craddock was trying to overcome in his inductive method, which he introduced to homiletics in his book, *As One Without Authority*.[11] Craddock was seeking a coherence between what happened in the preacher's study and what happens in the pulpit. Craddock wanted the discovery process that the preacher enjoyed in the study to be replicated in the sermon. He

11. Fred Craddock, *As One Without Authority*, 3rd ed. (Nashville: Abingdon Press, 1979).

wanted the congregation to have the same "aha!" on Sunday morning that the preacher had during the week. The sermon method, therefore, replicated the discovery process.

In the end, Craddock still falls into the Romanticist hermeneutical gap. The sermon method is an explanation of what happened on the other side of the hermeneutical gap. The sermon becomes an inductive imitation or explanation of the process of finding meaning or understanding that happened on the text side of the bridge.

Richard Eslinger noted the problem of the chasm between understanding and explanation when he observed that even in Fred Craddock's inductive method there was still a "sharp delineation between exegetical and homiletical method." He asked rhetorically, "What if hermeneutics informed more immediately both the interpretation of the text and the emergence of homiletic form and movement?"[12] Eslinger is groping here, and in the end he veers off into a sort of narrative hermeneutical approach. Nevertheless, there is an incipient awareness of the intrinsic relationship between hermeneutics and homiletics, and of the need for hermeneutics to have far more to do with homiletics than it usually does.

In one of the most important textbooks for preaching in the last ten years, *The Witness of Preaching*, Thomas G. Long made an attempt to reflect the liveliness of the hermeneutical encounter with the biblical text. He organized his homiletical approach around Paul Ricoeur's description of "witness," and, in so doing, narrowed the gap considerably between explanation and understanding.[13]

For Long, the "witness" is not merely another way to say the "preacher" in preaching. Rather, Long develops the notion of witness as one who is sent by and from the congregation to the biblical text to explore the Scriptures, to discover there the truth of God's claim upon God's people, and then to turn back toward those who wait and tell them the truth.[14]

12. Richard L. Eslinger, *A New Hearing: Living Options in Homiletic Method* (Nashville: Abingdon Press, 1987), p. 125.

13. Thomas G. Long, *The Witness of Preaching* (Louisville: Westminster/John Knox Press, 1989).

14. Long, *Witness of Preaching*, p. 45.

Long employs Ricoeur's analysis of Isaiah 43:8-13 and the four claims about the witness that Ricoeur says are made by this text.[15] Significantly, the witness, in all its textured and nuanced meaning, becomes the link between explanation and understanding.

> At the point in the sermon development when the preacher makes the turn from the exegesis of the biblical text toward the sermon itself, the preacher moves from being the first kind of witness to being the second kind. The one who has been sent to the scripture on behalf of the people and encountered firsthand the claims of the text now turns to tell the truth about what has been experienced. The move from text to sermon is a move from beholding to attesting, from seeing to saying, from listening to telling, from perceiving to testifying, from *being* a witness to *bearing* witness.[16]

This comes remarkably close to closing the chasm between explanation and understanding. In the end, however, even the "witness" cannot do the job. The reason is that one has not even *been* a witness until one has *borne* witness. That is, merely seeing an event bears no consequences in this analogy until one tells what one has seen. Imperative to being a witness is bearing witness. The witness who does not come forward (cross the bridge) may as well not have seen the event. As integral as the witness is in the process, as coherent as Long's system based on the witness is, there is still an unmistakable two-part procedure. The witness first turns to the Scripture to witness an event, God's claim upon our lives, then the witness turns to the people whence the witness came and tells what has been seen and heard.

Long raises the critical question, proving the gap still exists, when he asks, "What sort of bridge should be constructed between text and sermon, and what kind of traffic shall it bear?"[17] Long's answer to the question is that the witness is the bridge — not between text and congregation, for the two are not so radically separated, with the text on one side and the congregation on the other. Rather, the bridge is between

15. Long, *Witness of Preaching*, p. 42.
16. Long, *Witness of Preaching*, pp. 78, 79.
17. Long, *Witness of Preaching*, p. 79.

the "text-in-congregational-context and the sermon-in-congregational-context." Long is trying to narrow the chasm. The congregation is the common denominator for both the encounter with the text and the preparation of the sermon. It is the witness, Long says, who moves back and forth across this bridge. In fact, I think Long is saying the witness *is* the bridge.[18] The traffic that is carried by the witness is the context of the congregation from the congregation's direction, and the claim of the text upon the congregation from the direction of the text.

Long attempts to capture the eventfulness of the preacher's hermeneutical encounter with the text by saying that it is not an idea that the preacher carries over the bridge into sermon construction, but a claim made by the text.

> There is an eventful quality about this. Something happens between text and people: a claim is made, a voice is heard, a textual will is exerted, and the sermon will be a bearing witness to this event.[19]

While a "claim" is less static than an idea, or topic, or theme, or pearl of wisdom, the claim is still the result of the preacher's exegetical work with the text. The preacher, on behalf of the congregation, hears the voice of the text, and experiences the will of the text. As the final step in the exegetical process, the preacher determines what the text wants to say and do in relation to the congregation:

> As the final step in the exegetical process, the preacher throws the first cord across the gap between text and sermon by describing the text's claim upon the hearers, including the preacher. We are ready to move on to the creation of the sermon itself only when we can finish the following sentence: "In relation to those who will hear the sermon, what this text wants to say and do is — "[20]

18. Long describes the move from text to sermon as beginning with a decision about what aspect of the "congregation-text encounter will be carried over into the sermon itself." While the language refers to a bridge the preacher must cross, it is evident that it is the preacher who spans the gap, even when the gap is the narrow one of the text-in-congregational-context and the sermon-in-congregational-context.

19. Long, *Witness of Preaching*, p. 77.

20. Long, *Witness of Preaching*, p. 77.

What Long has described here is, in fact, the classic three-step homiletical procedure: exegesis — hermeneutical leap — sermon construction. His method still implies the Romanticist hermeneutical dichotomy between understanding and explanation, but the "hermeneutical leap" is better articulated as an attempt to bridge the gap. The final step in the exegetical process is the beginning of bridge construction: throwing the first cord across the gap between text and sermon is the hermeneutical leap. While Long gives a new look to this classic model, exegesis — hermeneutical leap — sermon construction, he retains the time-honored approach to homiletics.

In a more recent homiletical textbook, *The Practice of Preaching*, Paul Scott Wilson detects the problem of the Romanticist hermeneutical dichotomy. Wilson doesn't bridge the gap so much as he adds steps to complete the process that he perceives is left undone by the classic understanding-explanation model. He observes that the task is left undone after exegesis, which he puts in the explanation stage, and so he adds "what experience says" and "what the preacher says" to the process.[21]

For Wilson, experience is life in the world. In this step, cultural realities must be taken into consideration along with the praxis axis, that is, what we know from the back and forth, give and take of theory and practice. The fourth step, what the preacher says, is the bringing forth of the new text, the act of proclamation. Wilson makes the case that the goal of all theological endeavors is to bring forth a new text, whether it is a biblical exegesis paper or theological treatise. Preaching texts should not be considered so different from the text production of other disciplines such that preaching itself is cut off from hermeneutics. This is a valid concern and bears insight into one of the problems of the discipline of homiletics in the past. The divorce between hermeneutics and homiletics has impoverished our preaching and left preachers wondering how to employ the insights of other theological disciplines.

In the end, however, Wilson is still in the business of bridge-building. He asks, "How does the preacher move from the biblical text to

21. Wilson, *Practice of Preaching*, pp. 125ff.

our situation? How can we know what connections are possible? . . . The process that we follow in making *bridges* between the Bible and our time may be named rather than left to intuition."[22]

Is there a way to understand the text to sermon process without employing the metaphor of bridge-building? Beyond our awareness that the horizon of our living is entirely different from the horizon of the text, is there a greater coherence in the text to sermon process than is reflected in two or three or four-step procedures in which we are leaping across gaping chasms? Even more, can we preach biblically from pericopes, passages of the Bible, which some of us would maintain is still essential in order to ground our proclamation to the unique and authoritative witness God gave to us?

Edward Farley thinks the answer to these questions is yes. It is a qualified yes, however. Criticizing the "bridge" paradigm that dominates not only the pulpit today, but much homiletical literature, Farley has set out on a path to define what it means to preach "the world of gospel," rather than the Bible, *per se*.[23] Farley suspects that the text to sermon process which seems to have required a bridge paradigm, not only does not produce biblical preaching, but hinders the possibility of biblical preaching.

Farley proposes preaching the world of the gospel, rather than the Bible. Preaching the Bible in Farley's understanding entails chopping the Bible up into discrete texts, like slicing a round layer cake into sixteen pieces. Preaching the Bible assumes each discrete text has something in it that is preachable, that wants to be preached. This view of preaching the biblical text leads the preacher down the slippery slope of thinking she or he has to catch, discover, find, uncover, *exegete* the meaning of the text. Once the preacher begins with that assumption, it is nearly impossible to avoid the bridge paradigm. It is nearly impossible to avoid the exegesis — hermeneutical leap — sermon creation schema I have already critiqued.

Ricoeur helps us here by maintaining that the text points to a world beyond itself. When it comes to Scripture, the biblical text

---

22. Wilson, *Practice of Preaching*, p. 164 [italics mine].
23. Farley, "Preaching the Bible and Gospel," pp. 100-103.

points beyond itself to a world where God the Creator is like a father who welcomes the prodigal home and like a mother hen who gathers her brood under her wing. The text points beyond itself to a world where Jesus Christ is Redeemer, where he waits and watches and prays while we sleep, and dies so that we may live. The text points beyond itself to a world where the Holy Spirit is comforter and counselor and appeals to God on our behalf, and in our speechlessness prays for us with sighs too deep for words. The text is not the goal in and of itself. The words of Paul, of John, of the prophets, are not magical words that when brought to bear upon contemporary life will suddenly make clear the murky meaning of our world or suddenly bring light where there was darkness.

The biblical text bears witness to the in-breaking of God upon our world through Jesus Christ in the power of the Holy Spirit, *and* it points beyond itself to a world in which God continues this redemptive work. By that in-breaking we are both judged and "drawn in hope toward redemption."[24]

To summarize this section, I said above that the dichotomy between understanding and explanation in homiletical literature creates considerable confusion or wrongheadedness at two levels. The problem at this first level is thinking that hermeneutics, or the step of interpretation, is one step within the homiletical process. Another way of saying this is that the first level of confusion exists due to the unexamined assumption that hermeneutics is the figure against the ground of homiletics. The larger questions and concerns have tended to be homiletical, and the hermeneutical step has existed within the context of these homiletical concerns. Or, again, the concerns of interpretation have arisen against the backdrop of homiletical concerns — how to get a message across to a congregation. This confusion, or misunderstood relation between homiletics and hermeneutics, has led invariably to the chasm, or bridge, paradigm.

24. Farley, "Preaching the Bible and Gospel," p. 103.

Second Level of Confusion — What Hermeneutic?

The second level of confusion we must address concerns the actual hermeneutical method that is employed. This is where the problem truly touches the weekly preaching of every minister who enters a pulpit on Sunday mornings. How exactly do we hear a fresh word for today from the biblical witness? We know that there are many hermeneutical approaches: feminist hermeneutics, womanist hermeneutics, Latin American and African American hermeneutics, hermeneutics of suspicion, and hermeneutics of consent.[25] How are preachers to know what are the assumptions underlying their approaches to the biblical witness? How does our homiletical process relate to our hermeneutical process? Are hermeneutical assumptions and processes interchangeable? If we are preaching in a narrative style, might we use any set of hermeneutical assumptions to hear the witness of the biblical text?

In order to straighten out the confusion, the first item of business is to straighten out the relationship between homiletics and hermeneutics. What we need is a figure-ground shift in which hermeneutics becomes the ground and homiletics the figure. Our grasp of a process of coming to understanding and a procedural method for coming to understanding (hermeneutics) must be the larger ground. Homiletics must become the figure against that ground. Another way of saying this is that rather than interpretation being one step in the middle of the homiletical process, the traditional concerns of homiletics will be found to be imbedded in the interpretive process, and the proclamation itself will become the last step in the interpretation process.

25. See, e.g., Raymond Bailey, *Hermeneutics for Preaching: Approaches to Contemporary Interpretations of Scripture* (Nashville: Broadman Press, 1992); Cain Hope Felder, ed., *Stony the Road We Trod: African American Biblical Interpretation* (Minneapolis: Fortress Press, 1991); Eunjoo Mary Kim, *Preaching the Presence of God: A Homiletic from an Asian American Perspective* (Valley Forge, PA: Judson Press, 1999); Donald K. McKim, ed., *A Guide to Contemporary Hermeneutics: Major Trends in Biblical Interpretation* (Grand Rapids: Eerdmans, 1986); and Christine M. Smith, ed., *Preaching Justice: Ethnic and Cultural Perspectives* (Cleveland: United Church Press, 1998).

Figure-Ground Shift

It will be helpful to clarify what I mean by preaching before examining this figure-ground shift in more detail. Fundamentally, Christian preaching holds the conviction that the biblical text is the normative witness to Jesus Christ, and that the biblical text provides an opportunity for an encounter with Jesus Christ about whom we preach. There is a long history of discussion in homiletical literature as to whether topical preaching — or preaching that is initiated by a predetermined theme or topic rather than by the study of the biblical text — can be considered biblical.[26] Or, on the other hand, can only expository preaching, which examines the development of a long Scripture passage but not the major theme(s) of the passage, be considered biblical?

Biblical preaching entails an encounter with the text, even though the sermon may take a variety of different forms, and though the function of the sermon, the aim which the sermon seeks to accomplish, may vary greatly. Preaching is biblical when it emerges from an encounter with a biblical text and faithfully discloses the world of the gospel of Jesus Christ to which the text points like an arrow. An encounter with the biblical text is that lively exchange between preacher and text where both preacher and text are subjects capable of interpreting one another. This happens as a result of our historical consciousness reflected in the "New Hermeneutic," whereby the biblical text is a subject that can read and interpret us. The lively encounter of preacher and text happens in opposition to the more one-sided approach where the preacher analyzes and interprets an apparently silent text.

Even in topical preaching or social and public issue preaching, which is initiated by an issue of current concern to a congregation because of its relevance in the ecclesial, social, political, or public arena, an encounter with the text is still implicit and necessary. Biblical preaching, therefore, is always a result of an encounter with the text,

26. See Donald G. Miller, *The Way to Biblical Preaching* (Asheville: Abingdon Press, 1957), pp. 26, 27; and, more recently, Ronald J. Allen, *Preaching the Topical Sermon* (Louisville: Westminster/John Knox Press, 1992), though Allen would say that for topical preaching a specific text is not necessary.

regardless of the form the sermon takes, or how the sermon was initiated.

An encounter with the biblical text does not necessarily promise biblical preaching, however, for the preacher may bring to the encounter a perspective or convictions that will not let the text speak for itself. The preacher may bring to the encounter with the biblical text only the set of lenses that belongs, as James Kay suggested, to the old age. Biblical preaching is Christ centered and Christ conditioned. It will be shaped by the cross even if the topic or theme is not the cross. Biblical preaching will be kerygmatic in the way Charles Bartow defines the gospel, or kerygmatic, expectation: "In Jesus Christ, God takes us as we are and presses us into the service of what God would have us be."[27] This is bifocal preaching, the ability to see both the world as it is in its fallen condition and yet at the same time the inbreaking of God's redemptive work in the world. We never look at the world hopelessly because we are confident in the God who began a good work among us and will bring it to completion by the day of Jesus Christ (Phil. 1:6). God completes this good work not for our own sake alone, but for the sake of Jesus' name. God would have us participate in bringing about the obedience of faith among all the Gentiles (Rom. 1:5).

It is not sermon form that determines whether preaching is biblical and it is not where or how the sermon was initiated that determines whether preaching is biblical. I can think of many situations where a sermon might not emerge from one singular biblical text. I have heard a few profound sermons from master preachers who seemed to take the whole Bible as their text.[28] But an entire preaching ministry cannot be sustained by such an approach, for individual books, stories, narratives, arguments, poems, visions need to be taken also as discrete literary units where the preacher plumbs their depths. It is from this disci-

27. Charles L. Bartow, *God's Human Speech: A Practical Theology of Proclamation* (Grand Rapids: Eerdmans, 1997), p. 49.

28. Consider, for example, Fred Craddock's sermon preached at Miller Chapel at Princeton Theological Seminary on December 8, 1990, on the occasion of the 25th Anniversary of the Academy of Homiletics. The sermon addressed xenophobia, the fear of strangers.

pline that the seasoned preacher may preach biblically at times when not using a particular text. On those occasions, the kerygma that is preached is deeply informed by the many texts they have studied and the whole message of the gospel that has been heard.

Biblical preaching, therefore, always involves an encounter with a biblical text. The encounter with the text is hermeneutical in character, no matter how the encounter with the text is initiated. From the time the preacher encounters a text for preaching, the hermeneutical process has begun. The decision of where the text begins and ends is a hermeneutical decision. It affects the interpretation of the passage for preaching. And the hermeneutical process does not end until the new text, the sermon, is preached. The preaching of the sermon is the culmination of the interpretive process and sets in motion a brand new circle of interpretation as the hearers begin to contemplate this new text that has fallen on their ears, and deliberate on how to respond to it.

The hermeneutical process begins with the selection and initial encounter with the text and culminates in the proclamation of the Word.

Hermeneutics, therefore, is at the heart of our definition of biblical preaching. Hermeneutics — the business of interpretation — is not so much a step in the process, a task to be done before "writing the sermon"; rather, hermeneutics is integral to and characteristic of the preaching task. The hermeneutical encounter with the text, that meeting between preacher and text, demands the preaching of the text. The hermeneutical encounter with the text is not complete until the text has fulfilled its destiny as proclamation seeking again to be proclaimed.[29]

Implicit in this view of biblical preaching, wherein the encounter with the biblical text is hermeneutical in character, is a homiletic. The

29. See Gerhard Ebeling, *Word and Faith* (Philadelphia: Fortress Press, 1963), p. 329: "The process from text to sermon can therefore be characterized by saying: proclamation that has taken place is to become proclamation that takes place."

major characteristics or components or concerns of the preaching task which have traditionally been the business of homiletics, are implicit in the hermeneutical encounter with the biblical text. These components include the purpose of preaching, the nature of the message, the identity of the preacher, the hearers and the context. In order to discern the homiletic, however, the figure-ground shift between hermeneutics and homiletics must take place. Rather than hermeneutics being a step in the homiletical process or defined by a particular homiletic, the hermeneutical encounter with the biblical text demands a homiletic. That is, the manner of our preaching grows out of the business of interpretation. It is the homiletic that grows out of the hermeneutic, not a hermeneutic that is placed in the center of an already-determined homiletic, or preaching method or theory.

The figure-ground shift between hermeneutics and homiletics is demanded by the problem we have articulated and addressed: the relationship between the three traditional terms of understanding, interpretation, and explanation. For all the recent publications on postmodernism or postliberalism, for all the debates over narrative, cultural-linguistic, or deconstructionist approaches, I believe the every-week preaching pastor is still here. The preaching pastor, especially when attempting to work from the Pauline epistles, is still stuck trying to negotiate these three traditional terms of preaching: understanding, interpretation, and explanation — or exegesis, interpretive leap, sermon construction. We need a hermeneutic, an understanding of interpretation, that has as its center the lively encounter with the biblical text as its foundation.

We turn to Paul Ricoeur for help. Ricoeur did not detail a hermeneutical method, though one can discern a method in his approach.

When we effect the figure-ground shift, homiletics will become the figure and hermeneutics the ground. The entire homiletical process will be nestled within the hermeneutical process. When a preacher chooses a text for preaching, the hermeneutic or interpretive task has begun. It will not end until the word has been proclaimed again.

This is how Ricoeur will help the preacher who is looking for a new way to negotiate the three traditional terms of understanding, interpretation, explanation — or exegesis, hermeneutical leap across the bridge, sermon construction:

> *We will find that interpretation is the yield that comes from holding in tensive dialectic the poles of understanding and explanation.*

We will find that interpretation is what we have when the sermon is preached, and that it is possible when we hold in tension the two modes of thinking, understanding a biblical text in its own historical horizon, and having a sense of its impact for us today. In one way, this redefines interpretation. Our interpretation of the text is not something we figure out on Wednesday and seek to explain or illustrate when we write the sermon on Thursday, then merely deliver on Sunday. Rather our interpretation is what we do when we preach; we don't even have an interpretation until we preach, or informally share the sermon in its nascent form with a friend, colleague, or spouse as the sermon is in the process of forming.

The process of interpretation is less like a treasure hunt with the goal being a singular discovery, and more like a journey the preacher takes with the text. In the old model the treasure hunt ends with the discovery which the preacher then brings to the congregation packaged for hearing. In the new model the process of interpretation includes the development of the sermon, the preaching of which is the telos of the journey. The preaching of the sermon sets in motion a new journey of hearers with the text, the telos of which is a new sharing, a new "proclamation" as hearers are compelled to share with others the good news that they have heard.

The new yield of understanding and explanation held together in tension *is* the sermon in which we are doing what Paul did: bringing the cross of Christ to bear upon contemporary life and seeing there what God is doing in the world, and what God wants to do through us when God has God's own way with us. When we effect the figure-ground shift, we will discover a hermeneutical or interpretation process that is lively, not static, and that ebbs and flows, or swings, between the world of the text and our world, instead of moving in a unidirectional flow from the biblical world to our world. We will discover an interpretation process that is textured and nuanced, not horizontal and flat.

In order to understand fully the implications of the new process to which Ricoeur leads us, it will be helpful to identify four working presuppositions or ground rules that will steer us clear of common errors and clarify the interpretation process in relation to other methods. These ground rules are to be understood not as rigid laws, but as guides or trail markers for the journey a preacher takes with a biblical text.

Four Ground Rules

The first ground rule is that as interpreters of a biblical text we cannot definitively know the mental intention of the author.[30]

This first ground rule has far-reaching implications for all of us who have ever found ourselves saying in a sermon, "what Paul meant here was. . . ." The claim being made is that we cannot psychologize or read the mind of the author. The text has been set free from the mental intention of the author. Once the text was written and then began to be passed around such that the author wasn't there to say, "no, that's not what I meant," the text assumed a new career independent of the author's intentions. In this new career the text takes on increased significance as its potential to disclose a world of greater reference with a limited range of interpretations arises.

An illustration from American history will serve well here. Ful-

---

30. In fact, Ricoeur says we cannot know at all the mind of the author. The mental intention of the author is completely inaccessible and unimportant. While I think this is an exaggeration, it leads us to an important correction from thinking that preaching from Paul is about figuring out what Paul meant and then applying it to today. Paul Ricoeur, *Interpretation Theory: Discourse and the Surplus of Meaning* (Fort Worth, TX: Texas Christian University Press, 1976), p. 75.

filling his presidential duty, Abraham Lincoln boarded a train for a small town known as Gettysburg in Pennsylvania where a particularly bloody and pivotal battle took place between Union and Confederate soldiers in the war for the American soul, and for the preservation of the United States. Lincoln would be responsible for a memorial tribute. He knew that another would be giving the principal oration: Edward Everett, a man known for his rhetorical prowess. Lincoln penned the Gettysburg Address in several drafts. Lincoln did not hastily scribble this address on the back of an envelope as popular mythology would have it; neither could he have anticipated the myriad ways in which the address would permeate American consciousness. He delivered his 271-word address perhaps even assuming it would soon be forgotten. Today the Gettysburg Address, far outliving the location, occasion, and limited intentions of its author, stands not only as a living word in American history, but a symbol for the nobility of sacrifice in war, the utter horror of bloodshed in battle, the agony endured by those who suffer injury, and the grief suffered by those who lose loved ones. Add to this recent scholarship which casts doubt upon the purity of Lincoln's motives in fighting for the freedom of the slaves, and you have a case in which the depth and breadth of contemporary interpretation may be far more rich than the original intentions of the author.

The first ground rule is that an interpreter of a biblical text cannot know definitively the mental intention of the author, and that once a text has been freed from the intentions of the author it takes on a new career where it has a world of greater reference with a limited range of interpretations.

What limits the range of interpretations? The text itself, which cannot mean everything, otherwise it would mean nothing. The range of possible meanings of a text is determined by the sense of the text: the grammar, syntax, and word choice. The sense of the text, of course, points to the author's intentions. The author said what the author intended to say. When the text becomes written and leaves the sphere of the author's influence, however, the text is no longer tied to the psychological intention of the author. The meaning of the text surpasses the intention of the author. In its new career the text has the potential to mean more than the author intended, and it is open to a limited range, but a range nonetheless, of possible meanings.[31]

We can see here how radical is our departure from Romanticist hermeneutics. Schleiermacher claimed that understanding a text meant having a similar experience as the author had in mind when writing the text. For Schleiermacher, understanding was a re-cognition of the mind of the author. He maintained that the subjectivity of the author was discernible through the objectivity of the text as it was formulated by given rules of grammar.[32]

But even Schleiermacher, later in his career, began to have doubts about the sufficiency of language to disclose the mind of the author. A shift occurred in his thought in which he came to think that the interpreter had to psychologize or "divine" what the author had in mind when writing the text. This came to be known as the "divinatory method."[33]

The first ground rule is that we cannot psychologize or divine the mental intention of the author, and even if we could it would not necessarily be the most important meaning for the word that needs to be preached today.

When we are finally able to pry our fingers loose from the security blanket of thinking that figuring out what Paul meant is the determining factor for our preaching from Paul, we may find the text freer yet to point to the gospel. When we are not bound to a conception of what Paul must have been talking about as the content of our sermon for this week, we may find a greater opportunity for the gospel to break into our world through the ancient, local, contextualization of Paul's thought. Is this not precisely what the Reformed confidence in the authority of Scripture is all about? It is not so much that the literal words on their face *are* the gospel, as it is our confidence that when these words are proclaimed again they give rise to *the* word, and the gospel

---

31. Ricoeur, *Interpretation Theory*, pp. 76-79.

32. Palmer, *Hermeneutics*, pp. 86ff. See also David E. Klemm, *The Hermeneutical Theory of Paul Ricoeur* (London: Associated University Presses, Inc., 1983), ch. 1, for a helpful discussion of "Ricoeur's Place in the Hermeneutical Discussion," especially as it relates to Schleiermacher and Dilthey.

33. Palmer, *Hermeneutics*, pp. 88ff.

is heard again. We are bound to these words as the primary and authoritative witness to God in Christ in the world. These ancient, local, contextualized words do not, however, bind God or God's Holy Spirit to antiquity. Every time we proclaim them again, in every new culture, context, and language, the Spirit of God makes them new and fresh in fulfilling the promise of the gospel: that the word will never proceed from the preacher's mouth and come back empty.

The first ground rule, therefore, is that as interpreters of a biblical text we cannot know definitively the mind of the author, and even when we can deduce what the author might have meant, it is not necessarily the most significant meaning for us today. Rather, it can only point to the realities of a fallen world and the ways in which God is at work in our world today.

The second ground rule has to do with the intended use of historical-critical methods in biblical interpretation.

The second ground rule is that historical-critical methods are better used to find out what a text does not mean than what a text does mean.

Since the definitive mental intention of the author is unavailable, critical methods are not used to reconstruct a situation in which the interpreter "figures out" what the author must have meant by virtue of the identity of the audience, the problem addressed, the socio-cultural-historical situation, or the literary style or genre employed. Critical methods may be used to establish the sense of the text, but even more they are better used to find out what the text does not mean as this critical exploration challenges the interpreter's prejudices and pre-understandings of the text. Historical-critical methods are used to establish the range of possible meanings that are consistent with the sense (the what) and the significance (the about what) of the text.

This second ground rule demands further attention because it calls into question a time-honored way of preaching Paul. Preaching what Paul meant is what we most commonly do when working from a Pauline text. How is it that we cannot know what Paul meant when what he meant is clearly indicated by what he wrote?

Ricoeur would attempt to steer us through the fallacies found at either end of the debate regarding authorial intention and validity in interpretation. He cites E. D. Hirsch, on the one hand, who argues that the author's intention is available through the author's written word and is decisive for valid interpretation. At the other end of the spectrum, Hans-Georg Gadamer maintains the author's intention is inaccessible and, therefore, not a norm for validity in interpretation. Ricoeur negotiates a fruitful way between these two competing schools of thought. He warns against committing what he calls "fallacies" at both ends of the spectrum.

"The fallacy of the absolute text" is thinking the text is authorless. This is what Hirsch calls Gadamer's banishment of the author. The fallacy of the absolute text is to forget that behind the text was a human author. One of the foundational building blocks of Ricoeur's hermeneutics is that the subject is the bearer of meaning. A human life is behind the existence of the text, and the language which gave rise to the text is the instrument through which a human author gave sense to an experience. "A text remains a discourse told by somebody, said by someone to someone else about something." The text is fundamentally a "human" made object.[34]

Gadamer would accuse Hirsch of the "intentional fallacy," that is, thinking the author's intended meaning is the one and only meaning that is valid.[35] Here Ricoeur charts a middle ground between Hirsch and Gadamer. He maintains that when a spectrum of meanings is gathered, the interpreter may have a fair degree of certainty that the author's intention is included. But the interpreter will never know with absolute certainty the author's intention; nor does it matter. Furthermore, even after arriving at a guess of what the author may have intended, the author's meaning is not necessarily the most significant interpretation for the particular context; it is only one interpretation asking to be heard.

34. Ricoeur, *Interpretation Theory*, p. 30.
35. Ricoeur, *Interpretation Theory*, p. 30.

It is easy to see how the interpretation of Pauline texts often falls into one of these two fallacies. On one end of the spectrum, in the fallacy of the absolute text, Paul is disliked or distrusted enough that he must be banished, even while we use for preaching selected texts of which we approve. Another way Paul the human author gets banished is when he is treated as though he were a robotic thinker at the service of someone else's political agenda. Paul the human author is banished when we twist his logic to make his words mean what we want them to mean in order to endorse the message we want to preach.

At the other end of the spectrum, in the intentional fallacy, all of Paul's words are taken strictly by their plain meaning. What Paul said is precisely what he meant and it is what he meant for our world as well. We may trust the signs and symbols of grammar, vocabulary, and syntax to tell us what Paul meant. Furthermore, not only can we know what Paul meant, but this meaning is then the valid interpretation for preaching today.

Ricoeur helps us steer clear of both of these fallacies that by maintaining the author is important and that we may have some idea of what the author may have meant — we can get a "sense" of the text.[36] But once the written word outlives and outdistances the author's ability to inform and correct its interpretation, the text takes on a life of its own. It has a public existence in which the world to which the text points may be appropriated by different people in different ways. This is not to say that any interpretation is as valid as any another. It is to say that a "surplus of meaning," beyond any derived from possible authorial intent, is possible as a given text enters into different relationships with different people.[37]

For Ricoeur the "surplus of meaning" refers to the conviction that

---

36. E. D. Hirsch, Jr., *Validity in Interpretation* (New Haven: Yale University Press, 1967). See especially chs. 1 and 2 for this discussion. In hermeneutical thought "sense" is something of a technical term. Ricoeur would say that what Hirsch calls the "verbal meaning" of the text is the "sense" of the text. This is the older "grammatical" understanding of hermeneutics, and is one adopted by Hans Frei in *The Identity of Jesus Christ: The Hermeneutical Bases of Dogmatic Theology* (Philadelphia: Fortress Press, 1975), pp. xvff.

37. Ricoeur, *Interpretation Theory*, pp. 36, 37.

when a text is committed to writing, it no longer belongs only to the situation of its writing. Spoken discourse is situational in character. The partners in a conversation may question and correct meaning and intention as the conversation progresses. When committed to writing, however, a text is freed from the direct reference of the situation of spoken discourse, and, therefore, free to project not just a situation, but a world of its own:

> As the meaning of the text is beyond the author's intention and beyond what the reader of any specific time grasps, so its reference is beyond what the ordinary world offers. . . . In reading it, man is invited to explore dimensions of reality beyond the limitations of his situation. So interpretation should not seek for intentions *behind* the text but explain the sort of being-in-the-world unfolded *in front of it*.[38]

There is a surplus of meaning, therefore, because the written text points to a world of meaning beyond itself, where more than one particular meaning is potentially coincident with the direction of the text.

When the text is freed by writing to project a world of its own, each interpreter is likewise freed to interact with the text on an individual level. Each interpreter will bring to the text a world and lifetime of meanings and references that will be a part of the interpreter's perspective as the interpreter encounters the text. In the end, each interpreter will appropriate the text in a different way, and the text will always have more to say than any single interpreter can appropriate at any given time. This capacity of the text to mean more than any one interpreter can grasp at any one time, is referred to as a surplus of meaning.

The surplus of meaning gives us permission to hear a fresh word from Pauline texts. The surplus of meaning gives us the opportunity to hear a new view of the world, a new perspective, because it gives permission for those whose voices have never been heard to speak. I've had many preachers tell me, especially women, that they had a word

38. Theodoor Marius van Leeuwen, *Surplus of Meaning: Ontology and Eschatology in the Philosophy of Paul Ricoeur* (Amsterdam: Rodopi, 1981), p. 87.

to preach that had emerged from a Pauline passage, but they did not feel free to preach it because they could not find it validated in any biblical commentary. The biblical commentaries they had consulted were written primarily by persons of similar background and perspective, usually white males of western European descent who had been trained in the classical school of German Euro-American biblical theology. It takes a tremendous amount of courage for one to believe that she has heard a new word from Paul that no one has ever heard before. It takes a tremendous amount of confidence in one's own biblical scholarship to venture forth with a new hearing of an old word, a new hearing to which no one else has given voice.

Ricoeur's notion of the surplus of meaning explains in part how a fresh, faithful word can emerge when a new voice is brought to the preaching task. As a consequence of this second ground rule, that critical-historical methods are used not to tell us what the text means, but to help eliminate what it does not mean, we do not have to find our particular hearing of the text validated in the critical source work. Rather, we can use the critical source work to determine if there are specific problems with what we are hearing from the text.

Our second ground rule goes a great way to free us in hearing a fresh word because preachers can go to the critical sources looking not for an interpretation to be validated, but to see if there is any reason it should be *invalidated*. The surplus of meaning found in the text leads to the third ground rule.

The third ground rule is that the text has the potential and power to disclose to the interpreter a world of its own.

The third ground rule characterizes the text as a subject in a radical way. One of the unfortunate by-products of the emphasis upon the historical-critical method is that the text has become an object of our study. The text is something we analyze, critically examine from many angles, try to figure out. We look underneath it, we look behind it, we often regard it as a mute dead letter. This is inadvertent, but it is one of the counterintuitive aspects of having a theological education that

101

many preachers never resolve. Many enter seminary with the devotional conviction that Scripture speaks to them. When it becomes the object of their study, however, many find Scripture becoming mute. Add to this a methodology for preaching that does not seem to rely heavily upon the Holy Spirit (as method itself is often understood to be antithetical to the work of the Holy Spirit), and the voice of Scripture seems to be at odds with responsible critical study of Scripture.

When we return to the conviction that the text is a subject with which we enter into dialogue, we find a critical methodology that is coherent with the conviction that God speaks to us through Scripture in the power of the Holy Spirit. The tools of the historical-critical method are dethroned, and we can put them into proper perspective. Confidence in the text to create a new event for the interpreter replaces confidence in the interpreter's exegetical skills to yield the new meaning of the text or the original situation of its writing. A new event may occur for the interpreter because the text has escaped the historicity of the original author and audience, and has taken on a universality in its sense. The text literally means more than it says, and points beyond itself to the world to which it refers. The text has the potential to open up to us this new world. The text is forward looking.

Imagine pointing out to a child a bird's nest in a tree. When children are very small, and their thinking still very concrete, they will look at your finger, not where the finger is pointing. It is an acquired skill to stand together, face the same direction, and follow the direction of the pointing to that which is being pointed out. When we work with a text for the purpose of bringing it again to proclamation in a sermon, we are seeking to look where it is looking, to see beyond the text to the world to which the text points. The encounter with the world to which the text points gives rise to the new event which the text has the power to disclose.

This confidence in the potential of the text to give rise to a new event in the life of the interpreter leads to the fourth ground rule.

The fourth ground rule is that the interpretation or understanding of the text consists not in the interpreter possessing

*the text or its meaning but in the dispossession of the inter-
preter's ego and narcissistic intellectual tendencies.*

This fourth ground rule follows closely from the third because
they both have to do with the subjectivity of the text, suggesting we
hold the text in very high esteem. Consider a relationship with a be-
loved, or a trusted friend. A genuinely good relationship with this person would assume a certain amount of mutuality, a desire not only to
talk to this person, but to listen as well. A healthy, growing relationship with this person would not be dependent on this person becoming
the silent object of your study, nor on your skill in figuring out other
people through some prescribed analytical method. A healthy, growing
relationship with that person would depend on mutual self-revelation.
Each would need to listen to the other, share honestly with one another, and be to some extent vulnerable to each other. Being gifted in
"reading people," having a psychologist's credentials in terms of understanding human behavior, and knowing deeply the other's background and the circumstances of the other's youth would all contrib-
ute to the depth of the relationship. But none of these would secure the
relationship if one used those tools alone to carry on the relationship.

For the preacher, knowing well the tools of historical-critical analysis and accumulating knowledge of the background of the Bible will
all assist in the faithful proclamation of the biblical text. But these
tools must be held in proper perspective. They serve the preacher's
ability to hear from the text a fresh word for today. They enable the
preacher to hear more faithfully what the text might be saying. The
tools do not, however, do the talking for the text.

The fourth ground rule, however, goes beyond holding the analytical tools in proper perspective. The fourth ground rule requires the
preacher to set aside the preacher's own need to know, the preacher's
own need to define the world and the text. In a sense there is a reversal
in the common tendency to want to grasp the meaning of the text. The
text must grasp the preacher. Even more, the preacher must be grasped
by God through the text which, with the whole Scripture, has been
given to the church as a means of grace. In order for the preacher to be
grasped by the text, or by God through the text, the preacher must lay

aside ego, false pride, and the desire to control where the word of God would take us. In order for preachers to be grasped by the text, they will need to lay aside all fear of being embarrassed by the gospel; they will need to be willing to be wrong. For many this may pose the greatest theological challenge.

I am keenly aware that when embracing the model I am proposing, different persons will preach from the same Scripture passages and arrive at very different conclusions regarding painfully contested issues in the church today. Neither my model nor method nor even my theological convictions assure uniformity in interpretation, nor should they. *Herein lies my confidence: that when we humbly approach Scripture as the unique and authoritative witness to the Lordship of Jesus Christ, when we seek to look together to the world of the gospel to which Scripture points like an arrow, when we are willing to set aside our political agendas in order for all of our thinking and living to be brought into the captivity of the will of God, then God can and will continue to work God's purpose out through us.* This generation may not, probably will not, see the resolution of all our conflicts. Our hope, however, lies exclusively in the power of the gospel to disclose God's will and work in our lives by the power of the Holy Spirit for the sake of Jesus' name.

Summary

We have effected a paradigm shift in the relation between homiletics and hermeneutics. Instead of hermeneutics being a step in the homiletical process, we have proposed that homiletics is the last step in the hermeneutical process. Preaching is the culmination and completion of the hermeneutical process. With the help of Paul Ricoeur we have found that holding understanding and explanation (exegesis and sermon construction) in tensive dialectic will yield interpretation, rather than interpretation being a step between understanding and explanation. The lively, conversational swing between understanding and explanation will result in a dynamic hermeneutical process where the world of the text and the contemporary world of the preacher are engaged in a rigorous dialogue.

We have proposed four ground rules which constitute the esteem in which we hold the text. They set the parameters and the terms of the preacher's relationship with the text. They serve as trail markers in the preacher's journey with the text. Keeping these four ground rules in mind, that

1. *as interpreters of a biblical text we cannot definitively know the mental intention of the author;*
2. *historical-critical methods are better used to find out what a text does not mean than what a text does mean;*
3. *the text has the potential and power to disclose to the interpreter a world of its own; and*
4. *the interpretation or understanding of the text consists not in the interpreter possessing the text or its meaning but in the dispossession of the interpreter's ego and narcissistic intellectual tendencies;*

we are ready to describe a new hermeneutical method, the swing.

CHAPTER FOUR

The Hermeneutical Journey as Swing

The method I propose is characterized by dialogue. When I have students write up their reports showing the work they did to prepare their sermons, I ask for a "Hermeneutical Journey Report." This has traditionally been called the "Exegesis Report." In fact, the critical work done with the text that is appropriate for the Exegesis Report is fodder for the Hermeneutical Journey Report. The critical work with the text, however, tends to be the goal for the Exegesis Report, while it is only an aspect of the Hermeneutical Journey Report. I avoid the language of "Exegesis Report" because I have found that students cannot avoid writing a paper that looks very much like that which they prepare for their biblical studies classes. The work done for the biblical studies paper is important, necessary work. It is nearly impossible, however, to avoid the bridge paradigm when the first goal is an exegesis report, and only then a sermon.

If we think of this sermon preparation work as a journey, specifically a hermeneutical journey, the exegetical work will be done. Every tool developed and refined by the biblical scholars can be employed and is helpful. But as we demonstrated in chapter three, this work needs to be put into perspective. Exegeting the text is not the goal. Preaching our exegesis is not the goal. *Preaching the gospel is the goal.* Preaching the good news of Jesus Christ, the redemptive mystery of God-at-work-in-the-world, is the goal. Therefore, I ask for a report of the student's journey with the text and sermon development from the time the preaching assignment is engaged to the final proclamation of the word. This journey takes into account such realities/entities/loci as local context, the occasion of the preaching, the choosing of the biblical text which will give rise to the sermon, the critical work done with the text (exegesis), theological reflections, the engagement of text and theology with the world, and the preparation of the biblical text for public reading in the context of worship.

The method I describe here is characterized by the kind of dialogue that is the particular task of the practical theologian. The dialogue is carried on between the preacher and the text. Once the preacher has defined where the preaching text begins and ends, which is an interpretive decision in and of itself, the preacher begins to become acquainted with the text.

Listening, Asking Questions, and Making a Guess

At this first step the preacher listens to the biblical text, which is the primary dialogue partner. It is a private conversation for the time being, though the preacher never forgets that the text comes from a world and yet points beyond itself to a new word and world. The preacher also comes from a world. The private conversation between preacher and text that characterizes the beginning of the process is a complex private conversation. Other voices may be heard in the background or in the recesses of the preacher's memory. The text itself may even call to mind other voices as other parts of Scripture are quoted and allusions or metaphors from other books of the Bible are engaged. The preacher will have chosen a beginning and an ending to the text for the purposes of preaching, but the voice of the larger text will be heard in and through the preaching text. That is, even at this earliest stage, the preacher will be hearing the voice of the larger chapter, the book, the genre, the theological framework and the context in which the text was first given life. The preacher will hear the preaching text in the context of the unity of the witness of Scripture.

The preacher listens to the text and asks questions of the text.

Imagine the first meeting with one who is to become a friend. Sometimes the new relationship clicks from the beginning and the conversation is active and dynamic. Other times the conversation comes a little more slowly. When the preacher converses with the biblical text in this early stage the dialogue may be dynamic and inspire in the preacher all manner of thoughts and ideas and questions. From the beginning the preacher might find the world from which he or she comes continually trying to impose itself on the conversation. These ideas and thoughts need to be written down. Images, stories, news events, conversations with other people — all these things need to be noted, for they may come into play later in the process. These thoughts are not to be denied as though they are polluting the process. These thoughts are the process.

The preacher listens to the text and asks questions of the text. Imagine this new friend: Where do you come from? How long have you lived here? What do you do to keep body and soul together? Do you have family? Where did you go to school? What are your interests? What are you passionately concerned about? It is a natural part of becoming acquainted with someone to want to know about him or her, to ask questions. With the biblical text, however, we do not have to worry about whether it's polite to ask certain questions this early in the relationship. The process requires we not only ask the most penetrating questions, but that we ask every question we can think of.[1]

As we ask questions at this stage, we listen for the text itself to answer the questions. We also acknowledge all the other answers to these questions we have ever been given before and all the interpretations we've ever heard or come to ourselves. This is the part of the relationship where you acknowledge that even though you have known each

---

1. In many respects these stages are similarly described by Thomas Long in *The Witness of Preaching* (Louisville: Westminster/John Knox Press, 1989), pp. 66-72. My purpose is not to retrace what others have said before, but to put it into a new context, a new perspective or frame of reference. Long is thorough in his counsel regarding how to listen to a text and what kinds of questions to ask. Paul Scott Wilson also provides a helpful model for the early listening in "An Initial Literary Reading of a Biblical Text," *The Practice of Preaching* (Nashville: Abingdon Press, 1995), pp. 133ff.

other for awhile (if the text is not in fact new to you), there is still much about each other you do not know, and even more, you may have drawn errant conclusions about the other person's character or personality from what you have heard from others.

We ask questions, we listen, and we make guesses not only about the answers to our questions, but also and even more importantly, about the meaning of the text, that is, what the text is about. To what does the text point? We continue this early dialogue with the text until we have exhausted the conversation. This may take one day or it may take three. Nothing is more important than staying with this first step in the process until the conversation has been exhausted, until the dialogue has reached a natural stopping point. The preacher cannot short-circuit the process by quitting early in this dialogue. If a preacher is pressed for time, this is not the step to cut out. It would be better to leave undone the more detailed aspects of the critical work that particular week than to stop prematurely in the initial conversation with the text (assuming, of course, a lifetime habit of the critical study of the Bible). This early stage is often where the sermon comes from. The early questions, the early inspirations, are where our own voice is heard. We are naïve at this point and willing to venture forth guesses and thoughts that have yet to be confirmed or disaffirmed by any other voices or those who would be considered experts.

This first step in the process, listening to and conversing with the biblical text, is the "understanding" pole of the understanding-explanation tensive dialectic that leads to interpretation. Having spent considerable time in this opening dialogue with the text, the preacher finds the conversation has fallen silent. At this point the preacher moves to the next phase where other dialogue partners are sought.

This next phase of the process is the explanation pole of the understanding-explanation tensive dialectic. Up to now the only outside voice the preacher has considered is one that would confirm the plain sense of the biblical text. Lexical aids might be considered if various translations have differed significantly or if the meaning of verb tense appears to be in question, or if there are other linguistic questions that would prohibit the progress of the initial dialogue with the text. But no other dialogue partners have yet been privy to the conversation.

109

Engaging Other Dialogue Partners

When the preacher opens the conversation to other dialogue partners, then many voices may be heard. Initially the preacher will want to consider those who may have answers to the questions that have been asked. These would include those who by formal training have become more proficient in matters of biblical scholarship than has the preacher: the biblical linguists, the biblical theologians, those who write commentaries.

I am consciously making an effort here not to elevate the importance of these sources unnecessarily. The work of the biblical scholars is essential to the efforts of weekly preaching pastors who have neither the time nor the inclination to become specialists at biblical scholarship. And while many questions will be answered when we include these various voices in our dialogue, we would begin to silence our own voices if we approached the biblical scholars too early with the attitude that they have all the right answers.

It cannot be stressed strongly enough that the scholars may know more about the text, but their voices of interpretation do not exhaust the possibilities for a particular text to give rise to a new word. Furthermore, the scholars who wrote the books are often not contemporaneous with our time, and are certainly unaware of any particular congregation or context. They could not possibly bring forth the word our people need to hear on any given occasion. Our second ground rule comes into play here, that beyond establishing the sense of the text, the purpose of employing historical-critical methods of biblical study is not to figure out what the text means, but to discern what the text does not mean.

> Actually, the step of listening attentively to the text and the subsequent steps of critical testing form a repeating loop in exegesis. We listen, then we test, but the testing sharpens our ears to listen again. Both the open listening and the rigorous testing are important, since, ironically, critical exegesis is better at warning the preacher about what the text does *not* say than it is at telling the preacher what the text *does* say. So we listen to the Bible faithfully, but if we

do so uncritically, we will often mistake the whispers of our own inner voices for the biblical word. If we only perform the critical analysis and not the attentive listening, we will gather data *about* the Bible rather than hearing the living word that comes through the Bible.[2]

The critical analysis of the text challenges the preacher to reveal and confront her own preconceptions of the text, her own prejudgments, pre-understandings: that is, prejudices. Critical analysis of the text may help us find where we go wrong in interpreting a text. Critical analysis will not, however, give us the definitive answer regarding the text's "meaning" for today.

The most profound instance in which this has happened to me was in working not with a Pauline text, but with a Johannine text. The occasion was a community Good Friday service to be held at one of the local Episcopalian churches. It was my turn to represent our church at this service, and I was assigned the sixth word, "It is finished" (John 19:30). In my initial conversation with the text I arrived at the conclusion that this was a cry of defeat for Jesus. This was simply his way of saying, "It's over," and there was no way it could be interpreted as anything but exhausted defeat, given that his own religious elders were behind his crucifixion, that he had been betrayed and denied by his own disciples, and even now it would appear that those who loved him best had deserted him.

When I engaged my dialogue partners, however, I found no one who would confirm this guess I had made as to the meaning of the text. I went from office to office of the pastors on staff at the large church where I was serving, looking in every commentary and critical source I could find. Not only would no one confirm my guess, each one explicitly named my guess and said it was not true. One source took an historical perspective showing how the church in every age had viewed "It is finished" as a victory cry.

I had a critical decision to make. I was convinced this was a cry of defeat even though every other partner I engaged insisted it was a cry

2. Long, *Witness of Preaching*, pp. 71-72.

of victory. Was I going to swim against the current and insist on the virtue of my guess? Was I going to swim against all of church history, the interpretation of the church through the ages, to insist that Jesus was crying out in defeat? Was I the one theologically-trained person in all of Christendom to insist that when it came to "It is finished" the triumphalism of John had met its match?

In the end, I had to bow to the wisdom of my dialogue partners, not because they were silent on the issue, not because my voice was the first to raise the issue, but because many had obviously asked the same question throughout the ages, and had arrived at the same conclusion. Even at the hour of his death, according to John, Jesus was able to acknowledge that he had completed his mission faithfully. He had triumphed.

The sermon emerged from confronting my own prejudices and judgments about the text. It was no small matter that one of my dearest childhood friends had died suddenly from an ectopic pregnancy less than a month earlier. The world was very dark to me at that time, and that darkness was the filter for my interpretation of the text. But that encounter is exactly where the sermon was born. Many of us cry in defeat at the precise moment when Jesus claims victory. The sermon is born of that paradox because the world is rife with that paradox, that crucible. The crux of the matter, the point of conflict in the paradox, the human cry of defeat in the face of Jesus' victory cry, "It is finished," is the new age confronting the old face to face.

We engage the conversation partners not to find out what the text means, but to find out what it doesn't mean. We engage the partners to make sure that we are not going in a direction which is *not* coherent with the text. We engage the partners not because they have all the answers but because they have had more time to study critical issues. If a preacher has a sense about the direction a text is pointing that is not disaffirmed by the partners, then that direction continues to have life. The preacher must continue to examine her sense of the direction of the text *and herself* to make sure that her thinking about the text and with the text is in fact in the world of the text, that it is coherent with the reference of the text, that the text in fact points that direction. If it does, even though it is not mentioned by any of the scholars, it becomes fair game eventually to be preached.

Countless times in my teaching I have had students who have preached what I call a "safe word" from a biblical text. The "safe word" is the word that emerges not from the confluence of the preacher's life-in-faith-in-the-world and the world to which the biblical text points like an arrow, the world where God is still about the redemptive work of God in Jesus Christ through the power of the Holy Spirit. The "safe word" does not emerge from the confluence of these two worlds. The safe word is that which comes prepackaged from a commentary. For some this is simply an early phase born of inexperience. More painful, as I have mentioned, is the testimony of women who have confessed they had a new insight into the text but since they didn't see it mentioned or confirmed or discussed in any of the commentaries, they concluded it was not a valid word. They concluded they must be wrong, had missed the mark, were out of bounds. In fact, what was happening was that these women were hearing the word in a new way and had fresh insight into the bearing of Scripture upon our world.

Three safeguards can be established for overcoming this commentary-bound way of viewing the Bible for preaching. One is for the preacher to exhaust the one-on-one conversation with the biblical text before moving to the commentaries and other critical sources. The second is to de-throne the commentaries and those who write them, viewing them more as colleagues and peers, dialogue partners who have a specialization that differs from the preacher's. And third is to consult critical sources representing as many different perspectives as possible. Considering work from different racial, ethnic, gender, denominational, and international voices will challenge our own assumptions, expand our view of the world and the world of the text, and often let those of us who are not from dominant scholarship traditions know that we are not alone.

What will happen when the dialogue partners are engaged is that some questions will be answered, some guesses will be confirmed, and some will be disaffirmed. Almost invariably, conversing with these new dialogue partners will open up still more questions and set in motion a new round of conversation.

Ricoeur thinks of these two phases of going back and forth be-

tween guessing and dialogue, and conversing with the dialogue partners as the classic hermeneutical circle. In the hermeneutical circle one
begins with the first stage of understanding, which is gaining the plain
meaning of the text, moves through explanation, which is validating
the meaning, and then completes the process by sharing the word,
which sets in motion a new hermeneutical circle.

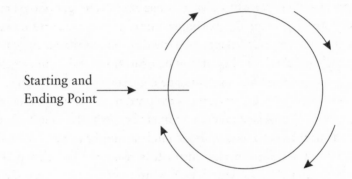

Starting and
Ending Point

Commenting on Ricoeur, Theodoor van Leeuwen suggests that the
better image is a hermeneutical arch.[3] Van Leeuwen suggests that the
arch image works better because the two poles are held in tensive dialectic and movement between the two poles is what creates the possibility for a new interpretation, a new word. In the construction of an
arch, neither pillar of the arch can stand independently of the other;
each pillar is held up by the support of the other. Van Leeuwen consid-
ers this the best visualization of Ricoeur's dialectic between understanding and explanation, with the interpretation being the yield of
this tensive dialectic (see the figure on p. 115). I like van Leeuwen's
reasoning and I think he is right that the arch is a good image. The
problem with the circle is that it is too neat, giving the impression that
one moves steadily around the circle. The problem with the arch, however, is that the arch stops at the point of going back and forth between
the two poles of understanding and explanation.

3. Theodoor van Leeuwen, *Surplus of Meaning: Ontology and Eschatology in
the Philosophy of Paul Ricoeur* (Amsterdam: Rodopi, 1981), pp. 90, 91.

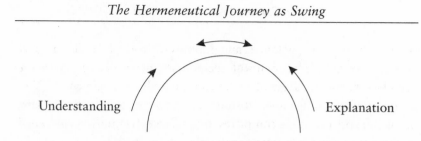

Understanding   Explanation

I propose the image of a swing. It has the advantages of the arch in terms of tensive dialectic. But even more, it has movement, and it holds the possibility that when gathering enough momentum, the swing will go full circle. Because none of us hopes this will ever actually happen to us on a swing, imagine a gymnast on the high bar. The gymnast creates an arch, essentially the bottom half of the circle, as the gymnast swings. When enough momentum has been gathered, the gymnast completes "a giant," a full circle around the bar. The natural movement of swinging back and forth is what the preacher is doing when engaging the dialogue partners and then going back and re-engaging the text in a one-on-one dialogue.

Engaging Text   Engaging
One-on-One   Dialogue
                                                 Partners

On one side of this swing is understanding, the grasping of possible meanings of a text: what this text might be doing, what the possible intention of the text is, where the text is pointing. The understanding side of the swing is where the guesses are made and the questions asked. When that stage has been temporarily exhausted, the preacher is propelled to the other side of the swing, which is explanation. The explanation side of the swing is where the dialogue partners are engaged, answers to questions are pursued, where the preacher attempts to validate the guesses either by direct confirmation or by finding there is nothing to prevent that particular guess from being valid.

I prefer the image of the swing because there is a repeated back and forth motion. The circle and the arch are too static and do not, in fact, best represent how most preachers work. The movement from guess (understanding) to validation (explanation) to interpretation to be shared (preaching) is not a linear, unidirectional movement. There is a back and forth movement as the preacher plays with various ideas, tries out various notions as to the direction of the text for a particular congregation for this time and place and circumstance, and continues to seek out still other conversation partners with whom to engage in dialogue. Often there are several, even many, possible guesses as to the direction of a text. One of the most difficult tasks in sermon preparation is to discern which possible direction to take when preparing the sermon. The preacher must forsake many good ideas in order to make clear one proclamation on any given Sunday. This happens because the text points beyond itself to a world of meaning, not a singular interpretation. Even more than a world of meaning, the text points beyond itself to a world, a world in which God is at work to redeem all of creation.

The Swing in Action

The back and forth nature of the two poles of the swing are best illustrated in a sermon that emerged from Acts of the Apostles, but came to be a sermon from Paul. The text was Acts 20:7-12, the story of the young man Eutychus, who fell from a third-story window while listening to Paul talk all night.

Eutychus — Acts 20:7-12

On the first day of the week, when we met to break bread, Paul was holding a discussion with them; since he intended to leave the next day, he continued speaking until midnight. There were many lamps in the room upstairs where we were meeting. A young man named Eutychus, who was sitting in the window, began to sink off into a deep sleep while Paul talked still longer. Overcome by sleep, he fell to the ground three floors below and was picked up dead. But Paul went down, and bending over him took him in his arms, and said, "Do not be alarmed, for his life is in him." Then Paul went upstairs, and after he had broken bread and eaten, he continued to converse with them until dawn; then he left. Meanwhile they had taken the boy away alive and were not a little comforted.

I chose this text out of sheer curiosity. The story had been mildly amusing to me, but more than that I was curious about what it was doing in Acts. Clearly Paul was on the move, and it seemed this story was stuck into the middle of the action almost as a fond memory.

Listening, Asking Questions, Making Guesses

My first impulse about this text was that there must have been something of supreme importance for Paul to speak all night in Troas. I thought I would find the message or sermon, or a reference to it somewhere else in Acts or one of Paul's epistles. I had never come across it before, but I allowed for the possibility that it was there and I had missed it. Some of my other guesses were that

- this was a healing story;
- the author couldn't resist putting it in as a funny aside — "Theophilus, you wouldn't believe what happened to Paul on his way to Assos!"
- the story had something to do with Paul's journey;
- the significance of the story lay in the reference to worship, fellowship, or breaking bread together.

These were my primary observations and hunches about the text. I also noticed that after Eutychus was taken up alive, the people, all like sheep, were led by Paul back to the room upstairs to continue fellowship until the break of day. This was exceedingly odd to me.

117

Engaging Other Dialogue Partners

When I opened the conversation to my dialogue partners I was surprised with what I found. My primary hunch, that Paul's message that night in Troas was so important I would find references to it elsewhere, was not confirmed. Nowhere in Acts or in the Pauline corpus was there even a remote reference to the night Eutychus fell out the window. I was immediately discouraged from thinking this hunch had any further import for my work with this text.

A healing story — I was not the first one to venture this guess. My dialogue partners were somewhat divided as to whether this was a healing story.[4] Some said the story was in Acts simply to show that it was not only Peter who conducted miraculous healings such as with Dorcas (Acts 9:36-43), but that Paul healed people as well. Others said the Eutychus story was not a healing story. Healing stories in the book of Acts are formulaic: one of the apostles calls upon the Holy Spirit, the person in need of healing is miraculously restored, and God is then given all the praise and glory. The Eutychus story did not fit this model. Paul did not call upon the Holy Spirit; there is nothing to suggest a miraculous restoration, and there was no praise and thanksgiving to God. Rather, Paul simply assured everyone that Eutychus was still alive, and they returned to the room upstairs. The Greek indicates that Paul threw himself upon Eutychus, inclining most biblical scholars to think that Paul gave Eutychus a form of artificial respiration. Perhaps Eutychus merely had the wind knocked out of him. I did not think the healing story direction for preaching compelling.

A funny aside — None of my dialogue partners mentioned this possibility. I continued to be amused by the notion that the night was so memorable, Luke just had to tell Theophilus about it. I did, how-

---

4. See, e.g., Ernst Haenchen, *The Acts of the Apostles* (Philadelphia: Westminster Press, 1971), p. 586; Henry Chadwick, ed., *The Acts of the Apostles*, Harper's New Testament Commentaries (New York: Harper & Row, 1957), p. 230; George Arthur Buttrick, ed., *The Interpreter's Bible* (Nashville: Abingdon Press, 1984), pp. 267, 268; Johannes Munck, *The Acts of the Apostles*, Anchor Bible 31 (New York: Doubleday, 1967); J. W. Packer, *Acts of the Apostles* (Cambridge: Cambridge University Press, 1966), pp. 169, 170.

ever, search sermon collections and indices to find how others had preached this text. If many have preached the Eutychus story, very few of these sermons have found their way to the collections or indices. All the sermons I found used the text as a launching pad to expound on why we must organize our time better, or to condemn the dullness of the pulpit.[5] While the story still seemed a funny aside, time management was certainly not a preaching possibility for me. Such a sermon would definitely remain in the old age, *kata-sarka*.

Something to do with the journey — I found nothing in any biblical resources suggesting that this night in Troas had any effect on Paul's missionary efforts, nor did it in any way alter his plans. Much is made of Paul's larger travel plans, and that from Acts 20:1-6 we cannot tell what is happening to Paul as he traveled. It is not mentioned, for example, that he was traveling from city to city to collect money for the poor in Jerusalem.[6] As a matter of fact, Paul had spent several days in Troas and nothing of his activity in those days is mentioned. This guess is eliminated from any preaching possibility.

Worship, fellowship, or breaking bread together — Several dialogue partners suggested that this was the first unambiguous evidence we have in the book of Acts that the early Christians gathered on the first day of the week for fellowship and the breaking of bread. Some asked exactly what kind of meal was being shared — whether it was a social meal corresponding to the fellowship-meal which may have been at the heart of the problems in Corinth, or had Paul already become skittish about the fellowship-meal and separated the Eucharist from any other fellowship over food?[7] Additionally, Paul "was holding a discussion with them." The text does not say that Paul was preaching, but it does say that since Paul was leaving the next day, he talked with them late into the night. The emphasis on the Eucharist remained a preaching possibility, therefore, yet the Eucharist did not seem to be at the center of the story. Furthermore, it was not compelling for me.

5. See, e.g., David H. C. Read, "The Perils of Preaching," *Princeton Seminary Bulletin*, n.s., 6, no. 3 (1985): 168-78.

6. Buttrick, *Interpreter's Bible*, p. 264.

7. Chadwick, *Acts of the Apostles*, p. 230.

While my first guesses were not confirmed, I found other bits of information that helped put the story in context. It turns out that Eutychus had the best seat in the house. The oil lamps that lighted the room produced a great deal of smoke,[8] so in addition to it being late, and perhaps crowded, the room would have been very smoky. The person in the window seat got the freshest air. The swing was moving back towards my conversation with the text.

More Listening, Asking Questions, Making Guesses

I still wanted to know what Paul had said that night; I wanted to know what he was talking about. The book of Acts is littered with sermons, yet there is no reference to the nature of Paul's discussion with the Christians in Troas. If they stayed up all night to converse with Paul, what were they talking about? What was so compelling for them? I realized that *what spoke most loudly to me in this story was not what was said, but what was left unsaid.* Who were these people? Was Paul an old friend to them or a visiting dignitary? It seemed to me that the crux of the matter, the power of the gospel, was found in the unspoken story of these people's devotion to an all-nighter with the apostle Paul.

I also began to wonder if Eutychus was significant elsewhere. Again, I couldn't remember reading about him elsewhere in Acts or in Paul's epistles, but it was worth a try. I asked, who is Eutychus, and why is he important? Often a person's significance can be glimpsed by the meaning of the person's name: what is the meaning of the name "Eutychus"? With these questions I swung back to my dialogue partners.

Engaging Dialogue Partners

My dialogue partners confirmed that Paul was important to the Christians in Troas because he was probably the first to share with them the gospel. They were the recipients of his missionary efforts, and the ef-

---

8. Chadwick, *Acts of the Apostles,* p. 230.

forts of those who followed Paul. It was also mentioned that these were working-class people. These were people who had most likely worked the first day of the week, and they would be back at work the second day of the week. The Christians in Troas held no other significance for the journeys or missionary efforts of Paul.

I also received confirmation from my dialogue partners that Eutychus had no other biblical significance than this one story in Acts 20. I hit pay dirt, however, on the meaning of the name "Eutychus." "ευ" is the neuter form of "ευσ," which means "good or well." The second part of the name ("tychus") is derived from "τευχω," which means "to make ready, or bring to pass." In adverb form, "τευχω" means "perhaps" or "by accident." "Eutychus," therefore, is a well-fated or a fortunate young man. In other words, Eutychus was a lucky guy! Perhaps he had a window seat because he was a lucky guy. Perhaps he was taken up alive because he was a lucky guy. In any case, if Eutychus was lucky, it seemed to indicate that his was not a healing story. Alternatively, some scholars maintained that "Eutychus" was a common name and no significance should be given to the meaning, "lucky fellow."[9] The swing was moving back to my conversation with the text.

More Listening, Asking Questions, Making Guesses

There was no need of further information . . . or so I thought. I had listened well to my dialogue partners. It occurred to me that perhaps this text did not want to preach. But I couldn't resolve the question that had nagged me from the very beginning: What is this story doing in Acts? Only now my question was simply, What is this story doing? How is the story functioning? What is it pointing to? It was clear what the story was doing to me. I had a growing affinity for the people who had stayed up all night with Paul. But I couldn't figure out what the story was doing in Acts. If it was there to show Paul performing miraculous healings, that didn't account for the muted way the story was told. Rather, Acts 20:1-12 might have been a travel diary, the large outline of

9. Haenchen, *Acts of the Apostles*, p. 586.

121

Paul's itinerary as he moved toward Jerusalem. I could find no evidence of the nature of the conversation or preaching that happened that night. I was wholly intrigued that after what must have been the frightening experience of watching Eutychus fall out of the window, these people went back to the room upstairs, broke bread, and continued with Paul until the break of day. I knew nothing about these people; yet I knew them. These were people who were taken with the gospel. These were people whose lives were as broken as mine and those around me. These were people who had found the one thing that could make sense of their lives, the cross; and the one person who could deliver them from the sorry circumstances of life in this world, Jesus Christ.

Two common mistakes in preaching are (1) over-identifying ourselves with biblical characters, people, and times; and (2) not identifying closely enough with biblical characters, people, and times. It is too easy to collapse the horizon of our living into that of biblical times and easily say, "we are just like them." No, in many ways we are not just like them. Most of us in North America and the congregations to whom we preach are not Hebrew descendents. We are primarily Gentiles. We are not shocked by what shocked first-century Jews living in Palestine. In our domestication of a gospel two thousand years old, we have flattened the scandal of the cross and we are blind to the scandal of the particularity of the incarnation. We are, by and large, not descendents of a people constantly overrun by neighbors; and only our African American and perhaps some immigrant brothers and sisters have any ethnic memory of captivity. In these and many more ways we are not at all like the people of biblical times. We miss the radical nature of the gospel when we too easily collapse the distance.

Yet, in many ways we are much like people of biblical times. When I reflect on the Christians in Troas who blew a night's sleep conversing with Paul, I know what it cost them. We know how much it costs those beyond twenty-five years old who stay up all night and yet have to keep functioning the next day. We know what it is like to live in a world without hope, where there is no grace, no mercy. We know what it is like to live in a world where we have to secure our own future. We know from what the gospel of Jesus Christ saves us. In this way, we are much like those first-century Christians.

I felt an affinity with the people of Troas. As I dwelt still longer with the text, I imagined what would keep me in that upper room all night. I began to wonder what Paul had been doing and what he had been thinking, what he might have been talking about. I remembered in one of my conversations with my dialogue partners reading about the relation in time of this story to when Paul had written his various letters. I went back to my dialogue partners to check this out.

The momentum of the swinging had increased. There is a kinetic sense to the movement from conversation with the biblical text to conversation with the dialogue partners when the preacher is getting ready to swing over the bar. The world of the text is open before the preacher, yet there is a compelling direction pulling the preacher toward a focused word to be preached from the text for this particular Sunday.

Engaging Dialogue Partners

It turns out that during this part of Paul's missionary journey, the apostle was relatively fresh from three months in Corinth, where he wrote his letter to the Christians at Rome.[10] I began to imagine Paul responding to the needs and questions of the people in Troas in relation to the letter to the Romans. Wondering if he might have used phrases and themes from Romans as he talked about the good news of Jesus Christ and as he responded to their questions and what we call today "pastoral concerns," I began to reread Romans listening for a word that spoke to the kind of world *we do share* with the Christians in Troas. The story was functioning as an arrow, pointing to a world where people will gladly sacrifice sleep in order to be fed real food. These same people will not be deterred by one of their members falling out a window. They will simply scoop him back up and keep going.

10. Packer, *Acts of the Apostles*, p. 168. This fact was available to me earlier in the process, but I didn't notice it. Mention is commonly made in commentary on 20:1-6 that Paul had recently been in Corinth for three months, during which time he had written his letter to the Romans. It wasn't until late in the process that I began to imagine the significance of this.

123

This story did want to preach, but it wasn't the details or the exegesis of the story that wanted to be preached. It wasn't a morality tale on time management or even the dangers of talking our youth to death. This story was pointing beyond itself to a world where life according to the word of the cross met the old age and transformed it.

The momentum of the swing had increased significantly, so much so that I felt cautious about the direction the sermon was headed. I had never preached so extra-textually on any biblical text. Is there any legitimacy to preaching from Romans based on a text from Acts? Befuddled, I consulted yet another dialogue partner, this time a fellow preacher whose judgment I trusted entirely.[11] After telling her the whole story and where I had arrived, I received an enthusiastic green light. In terms of the hermeneutical swing, I was beginning to go over the bar. In fact, I had tried out "an interpretation" of the text when I told my friend about it. I had shared my appropriation of the text with another and found that not only was my appropriation of the text coherent with the direction of the text, but that the world to which the text pointed was compelling and clear.

Swinging Over the Bar; Completing the Giant (Circle)

My goal in the sermon was to awaken in the congregation a recognition of the same kind of hunger for the gospel that I increasingly felt as I lived with the Eutychus story. I had no doubt it was there. We live in a broken world. The congregation for whom this sermon was intended lived in an area that was besieged by leveraged corporate takeovers and buy-outs. They and their children were caught up in the rat race of over-achievement. The greater New York area was gripped by horror and grief at the story of a little girl in New York City, Lisa Stein, who had literally been neglected and abused to death by her foster parents. Grace and mercy seemed in short supply. It was clear the world offered none. How might we hear again with eager ears what the gospel had for us? How might the words of Scripture be heard again, as if for the

11. Thank you, Ann Hoch.

first time, in such a way that the words themselves landed on our ears and hearts like balm for the soul? These questions drove the development of the sermon. In a sense I wanted to do in the sermon what I thought Paul might have been doing that night in Troas. You can read the sermon in the next chapter. "The Eutychus Factor" *is* my interpretation of Acts 20:7-12, or more accurately, it was for the occasion of its preaching.

Summary

To summarize what we have done in the last two chapters, I note the following: in the Romanticist period of hermeneutics and shortly afterward, understanding was the business of grasping the meaning of the text by employing the tools of the historical-critical method. Explanation was the business of homiletics, explaining the meaning in a sermon.

In this new model, the interpretation straining to be heard is the result of the movement between understanding and explanation, between guessing its meaning and seeking validation through conversation with other dialogue partners. While we are still swinging between the two poles we still have only a potential word, a latent possibility for an interpretation that is not complete until the word has been preached.

I am attempting a major paradigm shift here. I suggested earlier that hermeneutics has been the figure against the ground of homiletics. Classically, and still in most methods, hermeneutics has been treated as a step in the homiletical process. The shift here is that the homiletical process is the last step in the hermeneutical process. It is not the case that we arrive at an interpretation of a text and then think of a way to explain it in a sermon. Rather, as we go into the homiletical phase, what might be called sermon development, we have a latent or potential sermon direction that is not an interpretation of the passage until the sermon has been preached. Even after the sermon is written, it does not constitute an interpretation until it has been shared in some form. Preachers haven't completed the interpretation process, the hermeneutical journey, until they have preached the word that has emerged from their journey with the text.

It should be noted that placing proclamation at the center of the interpretive process elevates speech and delivery concerns above the level of mere mechanics. The word which the preacher brings forth through this process is born of the faith that God has given us the Scripture as the authoritative witness to Jesus Christ and life in faith. The word brought forth through this process is born of the preacher's divestment of false pride and narcissistic intellectual presuppositions. In short, the word the preacher brings forth is born of a faith struggle in which the preacher must invest wholly and vulnerably. It dishonors the word of God when in proclamation the preacher does not pay careful attention to the mechanics of clear speech: good vocal production, clean diction, matters of volume, rate, and pitch. Even more, the investment of the preacher — heart, mind, and soul — in the message requires an authentic passion, an integrity that says, beyond the particular words, "I believe this. I've staked my life on it. Come and see what I have found."

The sermon preparation and the preaching that results is what completes the giant circle as the gymnast swings over the bar. A particular interpretive direction gains momentum, it demands the attention of the preacher, it becomes the word the preacher discerns the congregation most needs to hear this week. There are all sorts of compelling factors that lead a preacher to a particular interpretation of a text for proclamation as the sermon for the week. It is this compelling direction the preacher takes into completing the circle.

The interpretation process, therefore, begins with the selection of a text, and it isn't complete until the word has been preached. The final phase of the project results in comprehension and appropriation. The ultimate aim of our endeavor is to make our own what was previously foreign. The reason the interpretive process isn't complete until we preach is because the end of the hermeneutical process is an event where as preachers we say, "Yes! This is the thing. This is what I mean!" The word itself is eventful. Something happens in the exchange between preacher and people when the word is proclaimed. The eventfulness of the word proclaimed is what allows us to comprehend so fully the world disclosed by the text that we appropriate it for ourselves. It takes root in our lives.

When the eventfulness of proclamation takes place we are setting in motion a new event in which the word makes a claim upon the hearer such that the hearer must begin the interpretive process anew. Essentially the hearer has received a new word, a claim upon the hearer's life which demands some sort of response. Sometimes hearers go straight to fellowship hall after worship and share with one another what they heard in the sermon, what had an impact, why it touched them. In an elementary, rudimentary way, these hearers have already walked through the interpretive process. Even more, when the hearer goes home or to work the next day and tells another who wasn't in church what was heard in the sermon, then especially the hearer has engaged the eventfulness of the proclaimed word, appropriated its meaning, and by sharing that with another, has set in motion another interpretive event.

In preparing and preaching a sermon, one often becomes aware of a new burst of meaning. The preacher may have begun and finished the sermon preparation with a very clear notion of what the sermon was going to be about, but only in the proclamation does the preacher fully realize how potent is the new meaning. I believe this is a common experience for preachers, and making the paradigm shift so that the preaching is the last step in the interpretive process accounts for why this happens.

The converse can also be true. It is sometimes the case that the preacher realizes in mid-proclamation that he or she has simply been wrong about a text. It might be that the preacher has been wrong about the hearers, thinking they viewed or experienced life one way and not another. This is not merely a case of the sermon delivery going poorly. The preaching may be altogether smooth. Rather, one realizes midstream that the preaching is not coincident or coherent with the intention of the text. Especially if the preacher has not allowed the text to become sufficiently strange to him or her in the early stages, the preacher may not realize the misdirection of his or her interpretation until the actual proclamation. Preachers may be grateful, therefore, for the grace and forgiveness that precedes, attends, and follows upon our preaching efforts!

Doing What Paul Did

How does this paradigm shift and this revamped method help us to avoid the mistakes, illustrated in chapter one, that fall into the category of saying what Paul said, rather than doing what he did? First of all, before throwing the baby out with the bath water, we must take a final look at saying what Paul said.

Are we never to say what Paul said? Is it really the case that there is some inherent lack of faith or theological integrity in using the literal words of Paul? If the preacher quotes Paul, or even says, "what Paul meant was . . . ," does this mean that a fatal homiletical error has occurred? After all, in Paul's words we find major kerygmatic themes of the Bible. Are we never to say, "For by grace you have been saved through faith" (Eph. 2:8), or "We know that all things work together for good for those who love God, who are called according to his purpose" (Rom. 8:28), or "For I have received from the Lord what I also handed on to you" (1 Cor. 11:23)? Of course not. It is not that we must never say the words of Paul. It is that in our preaching we must do more than say Paul's words. We must bring Paul's words, as Scripture, into conversation with our contemporary world in such a way that a fresh word is brought to life.

In chapter one, I illustrated four ways in which we have traditionally preached from Paul's witness to the gospel by saying what he said:

> preaching Paul as though he was a *systematic theologian;*
> using Paul as a *proof text* or *launching pad;*
> deriving from a Pauline text a *kernel of truth;* and,
> preaching a *linear, rational deductive argument* using a Pauline text.

How does the paradigm shift and the method I have illustrated help us to steer clear of these appropriations of Paul's letters which may not be homiletically suitable in our contemporary church context?

Systematic Theologian

I have tried to demonstrate that Paul was not a systematic theologian in our traditional understanding of the term, and that even in more contemporary discussions of theological method, Paul's work would be better understood as that which a practical theologian does. While it is not fruitful to push on Paul the names of modern discrete theological disciplines, it is helpful to note the nature of Paul's work and the telos of Paul's work. We must continue to do the work of systematic thinking and practical/ethical thinking, and perhaps more of us need to be integrating the work of these theological disciplines such that the academy is not cut off from the church and the church does not starve for want of the work the academy does.[12]

Reenvisioning what it is Paul was doing will invite us to stop thinking of his letters as answers, and instead think of them as conversations. As conversations, that we still hold to be the authoritative word of God, we may have a better understanding of how Paul could say some of the outrageous things he said. When I allow Paul to be human, full of passionate commitment to the gospel, the Christ of the cross, I can understand how he would be willing to compromise the fullest expression of newfound freedom in Christ for the sake of the existence of the fledgling church. When I consider the sense of urgency to "bring about the obedience of faith among all the Gentiles for the sake of Jesus' name" (Rom. 1:5), and to do this before the imminent return of Christ, I can understand Paul not completing a modern understanding of social revolution in order to bring about transformed institutions. Rather than assailing Paul for not going far enough, it makes more sense to ask why he appeared to compromise what seem to be his own convictions when he suggested (in certain places and circumstances) that women should stay silent in the churches, and that slaves should remain obedient to their masters. Preach the urgency; preach the uncompromising conviction that Jesus is Lord. Preach these

---

12. My colleague at Eastern, Manfred T. Brauch, has often referred to Paul as a "mission theologian" because Paul's theological reflections emerged in, out of, and in response to the missionary situation.

things in the contemporary context of knowing Christ may not return tomorrow, and that urgency and conviction will lead us to do exactly what Paul did, but perhaps not always to say exactly what Paul said. In so doing we will be faithful to the Scripture, faithful to the word made flesh and faithful to what Paul was doing. If we were to preach Paul as a systematic theologian we would have no context in which to understand the conflicts between the kerygmatic, coherent statements, and the household codes, for example, which at least on the surface may seem to defy the kerygmatic statements.

The paradigm shift regarding how we understand Paul, therefore, is essential to an appreciation of the conversational journey we carry on with Scripture in preparation for preaching from Paul. Moving away from thinking of Paul as a systematic theologian is essential for avoiding the other three common ways of saying what Paul said.

Using Paul as Proof Text or Launching Pad

I am sure that many a good sermon has used a short sentence or passage from Paul as a proof text, coming in at the end of the sermon to give authority to what the sermon has been about. I have heard many sermons based on Old Testament or synoptic Gospel texts preached this way. The sermon is reasoned and illustrated in the context of the primary passage, but in the end one of Paul's kerygmatic theme statements is brought in as the final punch, the final proof that closes the deal. If this is done well and has internal theological integrity, then perhaps no harm is done. If, however, this is the primary way Paul is used, we form in the minds of our hearers a pattern, a paradigm, a way of thinking about Paul. Paul becomes the one who proves our case. We open the door to thinking of Paul as a modern systematic theologian with right answers that we can simply deploy in our sermons. We do not prepare our hearers for thinking of Paul's writings as a textured, dialogical message that actively interacts with a pluralistic world.

The sermon by Henry Sloane Coffin, which was excerpted in the first chapter, is a classic example of using Paul as a launching pad. The dynamic is the same as using Paul as a proof text, only as a launching pad Paul is brought in at the beginning. Again, Coffin's sermon is in many ways masterful. The use of Paul as launching pad, however, opens the door to the preacher saying virtually anything the preacher wants. The text exerts no necessary control over the process in which the sermon is brought forth (though for Coffin we suspect it in fact did). There is no conversation between text and preacher; the preacher simply uses the text as the springboard for what the preacher was planning to say even before consulting the text.

Working in terms of the new paradigm, both thinking of Paul in practical theological terms and adopting the figure-ground shift, in which homiletics becomes the last phase of the hermeneutical journey, will lead us into direct dialogue with the text. The sermon will emerge from our journey with the text rather than the text being only a fixed starting point or ending point.

Kernel of Truth

In many ways the "kernel of truth" misappropriation of Paul's writings for preaching today is similar to the use of Paul as a proof text or launching pad. The dynamic I am trying to uncover here, however, is that of exegeting a passage to find that singular meaning which then should be preached. This goes beyond the proof text or launching pad because it actually involves an exegetical process in which the text is taken seriously. It is the primary way in which the old paradigm manifests itself, the paradigm of exegesis — hermeneutical leap — sermon construction.

When I was in seminary we were encouraged in our Introduction to New Testament course to find the "key" to the passage through our exegesis. The key would unlock all the mysteries of a passage. Whatever questions we had about the passage, whatever inconsistencies appeared in the passage, whatever linguistic problems presented themselves, these would all be resolved by finding the "key" to the passage. I recall working diligently on my exegetical passages, reading everything I could get my hands on to find the key to the passage. I recall how frustrating it was to be told I hadn't found it. I never was certain I had found *the key.* I wondered how it could be such a mystery.

I was part of the generations of seminarians who took this training in biblical exegesis to preaching courses. We were given a method in which the exegesis of the passage was the predominant activity in sermon preparation. In those days, homiletical thinking held that an exegetical approach would keep our preaching biblical. In many ways it served the church and us well. And I am convinced we cannot preach biblically if we do not continue the diligent work involved in biblical exegesis. But we needed a broader context in which to understand the work of biblical exegesis, and a perspective to understand exactly how it contributed to the process of bringing forth the word of God from Scripture. In fact we remained confused as to how exegesis was related to sermon development. How could we think anything else, but that finding the key to the passage was finding the kernel of truth for the sermon?

With our new thinking about the nature of Paul's writings, concentrating on what he was doing instead of exclusively on what he was saying, and with our paradigm shift straightening out the relationship between hermeneutics and homiletics, we are able to put our exegetical work into perspective. We may find that particular passages present themselves to us with such force that sermons emerging from them may be thematically similar even though preached by very different people. The life experience brought to the text by the preacher and the radically different contexts in which preachers minister will give these texts a new voice.

Whereas preaching a kernel of truth leads inexorably to the old paradigm (exegesis — hermeneutical leap — sermon construction), the new paradigm and method will open the dynamic of life together in Christian community in which we will find the text speaking to our lives more directly, contextually, and contemporarily.

Preaching a Linear, Rational, Deductive Argument

In some ways this is the *kernel of truth* method writ large. Rather than finding a key or the main point through biblical exegesis, this method typically includes much of the exegesis, and the exegetical product is the sermon. This is not necessarily expository preaching, the best of which still has a primary focus and purpose for each sermon. Rather, preaching Paul's arguments normally entails the assumption that Paul is a systematic theologian, and that his hearers are interested in having their minds changed regarding doctrines of the faith. Sometimes the goal of the sermon is to change minds. And certainly there is a greater chance today than there was two thousand years ago that people will have some kind of Christian doctrine formed in their minds. The problem with this sort of preaching is that we don't all live the "life of the mind," and, while Paul at times may have been argumentative, his argumentation is never without passion and purpose.

The new understanding of Paul and the paradigm shift in which homiletics becomes the end phase of the hermeneutical journey will lead us to go beyond argument, beyond explication of Paul's argument to people two thousand years ago, to an understanding of what is at stake for us today. And what is at stake for us today is always a matter of the heart, not the head alone.

I have had the privilege of working in a Baptist setting the last ten years while also living and working in the Reformed tradition. My experience of these two traditions is that when we err, we tend to err in different directions. Some of us in the Reformed tradition, with its emphasis upon a learned, scholarly clergy, tend to err on the side of rationality. Some of us have leaned towards things of the head and neglected things of the heart. We need the passion of the apostle back in our preaching. Those who come from Baptist and other traditions that emphasize more the work of the Holy Spirit to inspire preaching may tend to err on the side of passion and emotion, without carefully and clearly thinking through the theological ramifications of what they are preaching. Many come to seminary needing the theological fortification to undergird their passion.

I have sought to accomplish a new perspective in preaching, particularly in preaching from the apostle Paul, in which engagement of both head and heart may lead to a more adequate expression of the gospel. Method is important. Method is not the enemy of the Spirit of God, for our God is a God of order, not chaos. Method, however, must always be subservient to our theological convictions regarding the nature of Scripture and the purpose of preaching. All of this is submitted to the power of the Holy Spirit who guides us and forms us according to the will of God.

In the end, we hold to the conviction that God is faithful. The word is heard because God honors God's own word, pouring out the Holy Spirit when the word is preached no matter the intentions or the methods of the preacher (Phil. 1:15-18). I join many who have dared to propose another way, and perhaps for our time, a more appropriate way, to understand the task of preaching, humbly seeking to be faithful to the high calling of proclaiming the word of God. It is with gratitude, therefore, for the preachers who through the years and over the centuries have sought to be faithful; to those whose methodological thinking has helped to sharpen my own and has advanced the cause of homiletical thought; it is with gratitude to those who raised me up by the preaching of the word that I submit the proposals found in this book.

May the gospel of Jesus Christ, crucified and risen, be preached, not only in word, but also in power, in the Holy Spirit and with full conviction (1 Thess. 1:5).

CHAPTER FIVE

Sermons

The sermons in this chapter are not "model" sermons. I'm not sure there is such a thing as a model sermon. Preaching happens in the ebb and flow of congregational life, and any notions I once entertained of preaching a perfect sermon were given up long ago. The sermons that follow were prepared for particular contexts with the average amount of time a preaching pastor might have to prepare a sermon. I say this because I always imagined that as a preaching professor I would have extra time to prepare my sermons. I have found that never to be the case. Early in my ministry I was given the honor of preaching at the high and holy hour of 11:00 p.m. on Christmas Eve. So seriously did I take this assignment that I began to prepare in October. It turned out to be one of the worst sermons I have ever preached. Months afterwards only those who knew and loved me best dared to ask, "Nancy, what *were* you talking about on Christmas Eve?" Even now, if I carve out more than the usual time within one week to prepare for a particular preaching occasion, I find that a sick child, or an academic version of a sudden death and funeral, take up the extra time I might have planned.

The sermons are formatted on the page in the way I format a manuscript for preaching. The formatting reflects my intentions for the oral interpretation of the Word that I preach. It is formatted for *my* eye; it gives me visual clues that make it easy to use the manuscript as a

135

tool, essentially freeing me from the manuscript. My eye can follow the flow of the manuscript more easily than when it is in paragraph form, and I am entirely free to be with the congregation as I preach, not "stuck in my manuscript." After a sermon is printed in this form, I will typically add handwritten marks, such as musical notations, for further clues that I can grasp at a glance.[1]

The first sermon, "The Eutychus Factor," used in chapter four to demonstrate the method I have been proposing, was preached on November 5, 1987, at the Hopewell Presbyterian Church in Hopewell, New Jersey.

---

1. For a helpful discussion of this style of formatting, especially as it relates to the public reading of Scripture, see G. Robert Jacks, *Getting the Word Across* (Grand Rapids: Eerdmans, 1995), pp. 209ff.

THE EUTYCHUS FACTOR

Acts 20:7-12

In the early days of my marriage,
> I was talking to one of my older brothers about this new reality
> > in which I found myself.

He said, "Well, how does it feel to be married?"
> I said, "Good, we like it . . . it feels . . . different."

He nodded his head. And then at my loss for words he said this,
> "You know, when you've just been married, you're not like the
old married folk, because they know how to be married.
> And you're not like the single people anymore, because you're
> > married.

There's no way to get around it. You're newlyweds!"
And I felt relieved.
> No longer was it a trite label for those married less than a year.
> > I felt my brother had named my condition.
> > > I was living in a new reality.

All the wedding planning in the world didn't prepare me for what it
would feel like 10 days later to be going about my business married.
> But my brother named for me my condition, and in naming it,
> > he affirmed it, and I felt known.
> > One theologian has said that modern individuals "live on
> > > scraps."[2]

Whether we know it or not we live on scraps of meaning.
> We pick up pieces here and there;
> > from pop psychologies,
> > from the ethic of the workplace,
> > from colleagues we look up to.

> We pick up scraps of meaning from the TV and movies and
> > songs.

> We pick up scraps of meaning from what we can understand

---

2. Don S. Browning, *Religious Thought and the Modern Psychologies: A Critical Conversation in the Theology of Culture* (Philadelphia: Fortress Press, 1987).

of our Christian faith.

And because we have a built-in mechanism which compels us to create a whole tapestry of meaning, we take our bits and pieces of meaning and we weave them together into a life pattern that serves to inform and condition our thoughts and behavior.

The question is, what scraps of meaning shape your life?

In a world where Christianity is only one scrap among many,

in a world where we bless the freedom to associate with
whomever we will,

to think whatever we will,

to say whatever we think,

and to worship however suits us,

who in our lives — and what — is most influential in naming us?

In a society that abounds with so much freedom it can choke us,

are we prepared to deal with a world that seeks to name us
according to its own rules, according to its own scraps of
meaning?

Because that's the kind of world it is.

It is a world that seeks constantly to name our condition by
giving us competing scraps of meaning;

it is a world that seeks constantly to tell us who we are;

it is a world that seeks constantly to tell us the rules by which
we are to live.

It's the world of the **CENTRIFUGAL FORCE FACTOR,**

where the speed of the spin of our daily grind throws us further
and further out and away from our center.

Like the speeding car that loses the edge of the road around a
sharp curve,

the centrifugal force factor throws us off center

and separates us from the ground we have always taken for
granted.

It's the world of the **BODY BEAUTIFUL FACTOR**

where style and appearance, or in homiletical jargon, presence
and delivery,

matter more than substance.

Flex the muscle, use the four-syllable word, be PC — that's
politically correct —

give the right answers to insure reelection,

preach what is safe,

tell the people what the people want to hear,

avoid ruffling feathers,

tell the boss what the boss wants to hear (no matter what
you really think),

and if you're not sure what you think

just say it louder and with more conviction

and people may think you're really onto something.

You can't fool all the people all the time,

but in the world of the **BODY BEAUTIFUL FACTOR**

you can fool enough of the people to get by.

It's the world of the **HURRY-UP FACTOR**

where we seem to have to hurry up for everything.

The *children* are hurried to grow up so they can get themselves
to school

and let themselves in after school.

The *young people* hurry up to finish school, if they finish
school,

so they can get a job and hurry into all the adult worries
we hoped

they'd be spared for a short while longer.

And those of us in the *work force* hurry to work so we can
hurry home,

so we can hurry the kids to the next activity

so we can hurry to lunch with a friend,

or hurry to check up on an ailing parent.

We hurry to make more money so we can hurry and retire,

and after we retire everyone else is in too much of a hurry
to spend time with us anymore.

And nowhere in this sickening cycle can a little comfort be
found.

And of course, *what is missing in all of this,* and I've only named a
   few factors
   — you could add more of your own —
   what is missing in all this is the humane factor . . . the
      community factor . . . the grace factor.
I look around myself and I find the world factoring out my life,
   naming my condition with competing scraps of meaning,
      most of which I don't even like.

There is another factor which our Scripture reading tells us about.
   I call it the **EUTYCHUS FACTOR.**
The Eutychus Factor also names our condition, I think —
   and it has a peculiar way of doing so.
It names our condition not so much by what it says as by what it
   doesn't say.
   And yet perhaps, just perhaps, if we listen closely,
      we may overhear fragments of Paul's all-nighter marathon
         conversation.

The story of Eutychus has been much maligned in the church.
   It's been used as a bad example of just about everything:
      from the perils of dull preaching to the awful consequences
         of not setting starting and ending times for your church
            meetings.
   In these latter chapters of the book of Acts, Luke indicates that
Paul has left Corinth, where he had stayed for quite some time. The
scholars believe that while he was in Corinth he wrote his letter to the
Christians in Rome.
   And now as Luke is depicting at breakneck speed the travels of
Paul as he journeys to Rome, travels that would rival the schedule of
any contemporary business person, *we come to a screeching halt* to
hear about the night Paul apparently talked too long and a kid in the
youth group fell out a window.
   What is this story doing here?
      Is it nothing more than an aside?
      Nothing more than "a funny thing happened on the way to

Assos" story?

Is this story really nothing more than a word of wisdom to
    those of us prone to preach communion homilies which are
    too long?

Or perhaps this is a little story to remind us why Presbyterians are
smart for sitting at the back of the church. That way we can slip out
more easily when the gettin's good. No, on second thought, these
aren't good enough reasons, surely, for a story to be in holy Scripture.

Perhaps this is a *healing story.* After all, that was quite a fall
Eutychus had. And the book of Acts is filled with healing stories.

Peter or Paul or one of the apostles calls upon the name of
    Jesus
        and prays the power of the Holy Spirit,
        and the lame walk, and the blind see,
        and the demon-possessed are set free! Praise God!

Yet, this bears little resemblance to a healing story.

Paul doesn't call upon the name of Jesus or invoke the power of the
    Holy Spirit.
    He just rushes down to where Eutychus is sprawled out on the
        ground, the people are gathered all around, and Paul
            embraces Eutychus.
    Some commentators even think the embrace is a euphemism for
        giving Eutychus artificial respiration.

I guess Eutychus didn't rate a supernatural healing.
    Is that what we are to conclude?

Worse yet, Paul turns to the people gathered around, this small
    house church,
    this intimate group of friends and families,
        and tells them to calm down, stop all this commotion!
    Eutychus is alive! "Come on," you can almost hear him saying,
        "let's get back upstairs."

And then a strange, a very strange thing happens.
    At least I think this is strange.
        Doesn't this bother you a bit?

These people, who have been jammed into a smoke-filled room all
evening,
these people who are working stiffs — most are not of the
privileged class,
this community who has just had the horrifying experience of
watching one of their young people, one of the members of
the youth group, fall out of a third-story window,
these people obediently go back upstairs with Paul!

Come on! It's Sunday night!
Most of them worked today, and most are going back to work
in the morning.
They came together as a small worshipping community,
creating an oasis for one another in the arid land of
scratching out a living;
they came together for worship and to break bread.
They were delighted to hear Paul since Paul was an old friend:
he was the one who first shared with them the gospel,
and he was in town for such a short time.

But Paul talked past midnight! He fulfilled a teenager's worst
nightmare: that if you go to church you might get talked at
to death!
He broke the rules which make it possible for us to invite our
friends to church:
yes, I promise it will only take an hour or so.
He talked for so long that one of their number fell dead asleep,
fell out the window where he was perched trying to get
some air,
fell out of the best seat in the house because of all the
smoke from the oil lamps, and he nearly got himself
killed.
And Paul, after nearly talking these poor people to death,
wants to reconvene their meeting once assured Eutychus
was alright!?

What responsible leader wouldn't say,
  "Oh, I'm sorry. I didn't realize it had gotten so late."
  Or at least, "Gosh, I think this is a good stopping place!"
What responsible parent wouldn't have taken the children home to
    bed?
  What good friend wouldn't have left early to give a guest a ride
      home?
    And tell me the truth now,
        wouldn't most of you have slipped out when you got
          the chance?
      Personally, I would have. I've left at intermission lots of
        times.

Unless . . . *unless* . . . there was something going on there more
    important than sleep,
  more important than their fatigue,
  more important than getting the children to bed,
  more important than running the risk of embarrassing
      themselves by falling asleep
    and snoring in the middle of church,
      or by being truly moved by the gospel in front of their
        intimate circle.

Why did those people stay? What did they stay to hear?
  What if they stayed because of the **EUTYCHUS FACTOR?**
  What if they stayed because they were in need?
  What if they stayed because they were desperate for a center
    which gave substance to their lives?
  What if they stayed because in their own strength they couldn't
    hold their families together by themselves?
  What if they stayed because they were hungry?
    There was no shortage of scraps of meaning in the first-
      century Mediterranean world.
  There was an abundance of would-be faith healers,
    spiritual gurus,
        perverters of truth and teachers of bad news.

143

But what if the people stayed — and their young people and
    children
  and friends and invited guests stayed with them —
    because their world could not give them a big enough scrap
      of meaning to feed their bellies and quench their thirst?
What if they stayed because even that precious intimate circle could
  not fill the aching need they had inside?
What if they stayed because in spite of the constant barrage of
input they were receiving in their data-base computer programs,
they were still dying of malnutrition?
  I wonder if they were as hungry as we are?
  I wonder if when the world was finished factoring out their
    lives,
    they too were left without the *humane* factor,
    without the *meaning* factor,
    without the true *community* factor,
    without the *grace* factor.
  I wonder . . .

What we know is that they stayed all night.
  And that continues to stump me.
  I wonder what Paul was saying to them
    and I wonder if perhaps his talk wasn't littered with phrases
    fresh in his mind from the recent writing of his long letter
      to the church in Rome?

Perhaps he talked about the one whose *cross is our center*
  and whose life is our unshakable ground.
Maybe he said something like,
  "You know, Jesus *died* for you. Why one will hardly die for a
    good person, though . . . *maybe* for a good person one will
    dare even to die.
  But God shows his fantastic love for us in that while we were
    still caught and conflicted in our painful past,
    while we were mired in the double binds of our present
    lives,

144

while we were as far away from God as east is from west,
Christ died for us! Anchor your life in him,
and no earthly force within or without will be able to tear
you away!" (Rom. 5:6-8)

Or maybe Paul was talking to them about the *temptation to be
molded* into what the world expects us to be.
Maybe he was talking about going beyond appearances to
giving everything we have and are to God.
Perhaps he begged them,
"Brothers and sisters, by the mercies of God, give it all, your
mind, your soul, your personality, your body as a living
sacrifice to God.
Don't be molded into the body beautiful the world expects,
but be transformed from inside out that everything you say
and do will be a testimony to the will of God,
what God holds to be good and acceptable and perfect"
(Rom. 12:1, 2).

Or perhaps Paul was talking to them about the *alienating factors* in
their lives:
the need to work fingers to the bone to make ends meet,
the diversity of religions and cultures within their own city
which made it difficult
to share their faith with a neighbor,
the enormous obstacles to being Christian in a non-
Christian world.

Perhaps Paul was telling them about *what holds us up and binds us
together.*
Maybe he was telling them about the Holy Spirit, the Holy
Spirit of God.
"It is the Spirit who helps us when we are weak.
It is the Spirit who prays for us when we do not know how to
pray for ourselves
or for one another.

It is the Spirit who tends us constantly when we do not know
    how to be a friend or when we cannot find a friend.
The Spirit searches us, searches our hearts and our minds.
The Holy Spirit searches the heart, the will of God.
    And then the Spirit intercedes for us.
    The Spirit goes to God on our behalf and with sighs too
        deep for words,
            he makes our needs known to God" (Rom. 8:26-28).

Or maybe those Christians in Troas were *hungry for that word
of mercy and compassion and hope* in the face of a world where
there was none.
    Perhaps Paul defied the logic of the world by saying,
    "If God is for us, who can be against us? God didn't even save
      his own son!
But he gave up his son on our behalf!
And so who or what do you think is going to separate us from
      the love of Christ?
    Hard times? Ill health? A loved one who walks out on you?
    A friend who turns out not to be a friend when the going
      gets tough?
    Do you think you've done something so awful
      it's going to keep you from God's love?
"NO . . . NO . . . NO . . . ," you can hear him saying,
"In all these things we are conquerors,
    no we are *more* than conquerors through Jesus Christ.
"Because you know what?
    There's not a thing in the world — not the **CENTRIFUGAL
      FORCE FACTOR,**
      not the **BODY BEAUTIFUL FACTOR,** not the **HURRY-UP
      FACTOR,**
        or **ANY OTHER FACTOR.**
    There's not a thing in the world that can separate us from
      God's love,
      given to us freely, graciously, mercifully in Jesus Christ.

And in God's love there is not a thing in the world that can
    keep us from one another" (Rom. 8:31ff.).

. . . But then, of course, we can't know that these are the things
Paul said to those Christians in the upper room during that all-
nighter so long ago.

And if he did say these things, they are still just pieces, scraps
competing with all the other scraps. Paul knew that. He knew we
never quite get it all together.

But I wonder. I wonder . . .

because the Scripture tells us that when dawn came, Paul went
    on his way,
and that house church, the small, intimate group of families and
    friends,
    the worshipping community left.
    They took dear Eutychus with them. He was alive and well.
    And they were each one greatly encouraged . . . I wonder.

HIDDEN LIVES

Colossians 2:8–3:4

"Hidden Lives" was prepared in January, 1999. I was planning to use this text as the launching pad for a series of talks at a women's retreat in California in March of 1999. I was acutely aware of the difficulties of Colossians, the complexities of translating "elemental spirits of the universe" (2:8), and the Pandora's box that is opened for many when hearing the household codes in 3:18ff. I felt led by the Holy Spirit, however, to deal with the difficulties women today have in figuring out how to make decisions for their lives, how to sort out their priorities, how to weigh the different voices that speak to us of what is valued, what is important, what is godly. I felt led to speak to the issue of where we find our lives.

"Hidden Lives," therefore, is topical in the sense that it was initiated by a general thematic goal. Once that thematic goal was in mind, however, I submitted it entirely to the biblical passage to discern what the passage wanted to say and to allow the passage to refine and direct the theme. In this respect, I do not like the definitive categorizing of topical and biblical preaching. It is my experience that a sermon that begins with a thematic or topical thrust can be, and perhaps ought to be, exceedingly biblical. It is also possible that a sermon that is initiated from going to a passage cold, with no agenda for sermon topic or theme, can diverge into a topical sermon because the passage speaks so clearly to a contemporary issue.

Pressed like all preachers to submit text and topic often before the sermon has been prepared, I did some initial work with Colossians in order to test my vague sense of theme and to determine the parameters of my text. In exploring the text, I started with Colossians 3:1-17, painfully aware that these verses led us right up to, but stopped short of verse 18: "Wives, be subject to your husbands, as is fitting in the Lord." I had no real intentions of dealing with the issues raised by this verse or others like it; I had not been asked to deal with it by the retreat leaders. As I explored the text, I discovered that I needed 2:20-23 in order to deal effectively with 3:1-4; and upon exploring 2:20-23, I found I needed 2:8-19. The text for the sermon became 2:8–3:4. At the retreat, upon request from the women, we dealt with Colossians 3:18ff., and similar verses from Ephesians at a special Saturday afternoon workshop.

The questions raised by this text have to do with what Paul might mean by "philosophy and empty deceit, according to human tradition, according to the elemental spirits of the universe" (2:8). What is this philosophy? What are the elemental spirits of the universe? What do these have to do with the rules, regulations, and self-abasement to which Paul refers in 2:16-18 and 20-23? It is clear that these things — human philosophy, elemental spirits of the universe, rules and regulations — have to do with the things that are on earth (3:2); and to these things we have died. What are these things to which we have died and how are they manifested in our lives?

Even a cursory study of this text leads the preacher to deal with *stoichea,* the elemental spirits. Even the translation of this passage has been contended by many. I had one of those homiletical "aha" moments when I read in a footnote in Walter Wink's *Naming the Powers* that the Living Bible translated well the phrase, "elemental spirits," as "the elementary ideas belonging to this world." This phrase is context-driven and therefore any attempt to nail down precisely what Paul meant is not only methodologically misled, but hermeneutically misled as well. The real issue is, what are the elementary ideas belonging to *this* world that threaten to take us captive? What is the empty human philosophy that so easily beguiles us?

It becomes clear in the sermon that the focus became "naming the powers," to borrow Wink's phrase. The sermon became less focused on what it means that our lives are hid with Christ in God. And, in fact, focusing on that which is above became a sort of exhortation in light of the worthlessness of focusing on things that are on earth. I consider this both a critique of the sermon, and an awareness that one sermon can do only so much. This is not what I originally intended, yet it honored my journey with the text and in my sermon preparation became inevitable.

HIDDEN LIVES

Colossians 2:8–3:4

I remember the day in early 1983 when the Dow Jones Industrial average hit 1,000 points.

The Dow had flirted with 1,000 at the end of 1972, again in 1976, and at the end of 1980.

But when it hit 1,000 in 1983 it was on its way up.

I remember where I was when I heard this on the radio.

> I was driving north on El Camino Real through San Mateo, California.

I had just left a traffic signal at Poplar Ave. near my high
> school alma mater.

It was still the afternoon, for after all,
> the NYSE closes early in the day California time.

This was huge news. It wasn't just an unbelievable high.

> It truly seemed to portend things to come. **Dow as God.**

Eighteen years ago I was delighted when the First Presbyterian Church of Burlingame, which issued my first call to ministry, equipped me with an IBM Selectric II typewriter, complete with changeable balls so the typeface could be changed.

This was a huge step up from the manual Smith Corona on which I had typed all my papers in college and seminary. With the ease of typing on that IBM Selectric II, I started composing my sermons at the keyboard for the first time.

Up to then, I had written long hand everything that I ever wrote, and only after at least two drafts did it get typed in its final form.

We were expected to be detail oriented. It was an embarrassment for a professor to circle in red a mistyped, or worse, an out-and-out misspelled word.

I wrote this sermon on an NEC laptop Versa 6030H with a Pentium processor inside. I have no idea what that means except that it is faster than the processor, whatever that is, that went before. My laptop can do way more than I can imagine and way, way more than I can figure out.

Fueled by investment in technologies, the Dow Jones Industrial average is now hovering at about 9300, three hundred points lower than its all-time, record-breaking high of 9643 on Friday, January 8, two months ago.

It has been a meteoric rise, a wild ride, hasn't it? And mark the day friends, because it may very well be sometime this year, that the Dow hits 10,000.[3] Truly a red letter day. And people are investing more and more money everyday.

We believe!! We believe!! Dow and technologies as God![4]

Of course, there have been some glitches in the market since that day in 1983. It has not been an entirely smooth ride and it has not been one of unrelenting ascent. When the market crashed on October 29, 1987, a few people killed themselves. *Literally*. If only they had known then what we know now. They simply would have bought more and waited for their stock to rise.

Friends, see to it that no one takes you captive through philosophy and empty deceit, according to human tradition, according to the elemental spirits of the universe, and not according to Christ.

We are constantly and continuously being teased and tempted, deceived, into making choices based on the standards of this world.

It is insidious, this deception that what determines our self-worth and our net worth are things the world recognizes.

Hey! Psst! Your self-worth depends on your Grade Point Average, your GPA! Your future net worth depends on your GPA, and your SAT scores.

Let's spend some of your parents' net worth in order to raise your SATs and do for you what your GPA alone can't do — get you into the college of your choice.

---

3. *U.S. News and World Report* (8 March 1999) reports that Alan Greenspan is not as optimistic. Unemployment is so low that companies may have to increase wages to find workers, potentially driving up prices and therefore interest rates and inflation as well. Is the best already past?

4. On March 29, 1999, the Dow closed above 10,000 for the first time in history, 10,000.78, to be precise.

The *New York Times Magazine* recently reported that children of well-heeled parents are spending up to $25,000 in SAT preparation courses in order to raise their scores an average of 100-200 points. Some start private tutoring as early as middle school for their college board exams.[5] Of course, you can spend a lot less, and still be spending a whole lot!

What are we telling our children? *GPAs and SATs are God!*

The not-so-funny part about this is the possibility that the relative value of the exam scores might be so easily manipulated by preparation courses. Of course, the more financial resources a family has to spend on preparation courses, the better the possibility of a high score for Dick or Jane. The exam, now coming under intense criticism, was intended to level the playing field for students from every conceivable financial and educational background, and so the article is entitled, "The Test Under Stress." Poor test!!

Friends, see to it that no one takes you captive through philosophy and empty deceit, according to human tradition, according to the elemental spirits of the universe, and not according to Christ.

Apparently, the Christians in Colossae and perhaps Laodicea were subject to teaching that would challenge the Lordship of Christ. It might be the case that "Judaizers" of the kind that Paul lambasted in his letter to the Galatians were on their way to the region of Colossae and Laodicea.

The Judaizers insisted that the Gentiles must become Jews through circumcision of the flesh before they could become Christians. And furthermore, in order to be Christians, they must keep the Jewish law pertaining to the Sabbath and all religious rites and rituals.

Paul calls the beliefs that would challenge the Lordship of Jesus Christ, "philosophy and empty deceit according to human tradition."[6]

Paul calls the beliefs that would challenge the Lordship of Jesus

5. "The Test Under Stress," *New York Times Magazine*, 10 January 1999, pp. 30ff.

6. See Walter Wink, *Naming the Powers: The Language of Power in the New Testament* (Philadelphia: Fortress Press, 1984), especially p. 67.

Christ philosophy and empty deceit *according to the elemental spirits of the universe.*

What challenges the Lordship of Jesus Christ?
    Everything from genetic engineering
        to the children's Sunday morning sports leagues.
    Everything that would have us set our minds, fixate us on
        things that are on earth.
    What challenges the Lordship of Jesus Christ?
        Whatever shapes us that is not godly and would be an idol.
We are talking about primary things.
    First things. Elemental things. The most important things.
        We are talking about that which has primary residence in
            your heart,
        that which takes up the most space in your soul.
We are talking about your first love.
    That upon which you build your life and by which you live,
        judge, decide, choose.
    The elemental spirits of the universe are elementary ideas
        belonging to this world.

And we know we are *selling out* to the elementary ideas
belonging to this world when we have just got to have anything but
Christ himself and his way with us.
    We contend everyday with manifestations of the elemental
        spirits of the universe:
    When every desire a child has for toys, tapes, graven images of
        idols
        (you know, lunch box, backpack, pool towel, sneakers —
            all bearing the image of the latest hero or heroine),
    when these demands are met in order to make the children
        happy,
        we are allowing them, preparing them,
            forming them to be deceived by the elementary ideas of
            this world.

When we constantly need the latest item in video, television,
computer, phone/fax/scanner technology in order to make
our lives more enjoyable
and our work more efficient
we are at risk of being deceived by the elemental ideas of
this world.
A few of us probably need these things —
the rest of us enjoy them as toys and, as often as not,
they get in the way of getting the work done.
We spend so much time fiddling with the machine we don't get
the work done.

I'm a teacher of those who now write their papers on computer,
and I can assure you that on deadline day the computer crashes and
the printer doesn't work as often as any dog used to eat a homework
paper.

The computer will check your spelling, but not if you don't click
on spell check. And you can easily edit, but not if you are composing
the paper an hour before it's due and printing it out ten minutes before
class.

What else has technology given us? The polls!
And better yet, instant polls! Finger on the pulse polls!

*Do not be deceived! See to it that no one takes you captive
through philosophy and empty deceit, according to human tradition,
according to the elemental spirits of the universe, and not according to
Christ.*

The polls tell us that as long as the Dow goes up or at least
stays high,
the status quo is safe.
The polls tell us that the country is living in two different
worlds, the world inside the Baltimore-Washington beltway
and the world outside the beltway.
The polls would tell us that as a country we can live with this:
that by the president's own admission he is a liar but not a
perjurer,

that he had sex with Monica Lewinsky but not a sexual
  relationship,
that he is contrite but not at fault (to quote Mortimer
  Zuckerman of *U.S. News and World Report*).[7]
We can live with this!

> To quote the author of Ephesians, *you did not so learn
>   Christ.*

I am not here to pass judgment on the president or even on the
process that has mercifully been concluded.

But we must not fall asleep to the reality that *the elementary ideas
of this world are gaining ground.*

We are disgusted with the details, but as a nation we do not find it
important if the president lied because it is only about sex.

It was just about sex. And as Geraldo has put it, who hasn't told a
lie about sex?

How is it that sex has become so degraded that lying about it is
unimportant? Truthfulness about sex in the context of a covenant relationship is as important as truthfulness about anything else.

To tell our children that this is unimportant is to sell them out to
the elementary ideas belonging to the world.

To tell them that it is only between a husband and a wife belies the
very reason we take our marriage vows in the presence of our family
and friends, in the presence of the covenant community.

> Because the vows we take are a part of the fabric of society.
> The truthfulness of our word is a part of the fabric of our society.
> We need the covenant community to support us in the keeping
>   of our vows,
>> and the community needs us to keep our vows as best as we
>>   possibly can.

Speaking truthfully and keeping our promise to tell the truth is at
the heart of our social contract.

> That is why a witness at a trial takes an oath to tell the truth.
> And not telling the truth is a punishable offense.

---

7. Taken from an editorial by Mortimer B. Zuckerman in *U.S. News and World
Report*, 18 January 1999, p. 88.

Jesus Christ is the preeminent witness.
> Jesus Christ staked his life on telling the truth about who
> > God is.
> Jesus Christ staked his life on showing us the truth about
> > who God is,
> > on living the truth about who God is.
> It cost Jesus his life. But it saved ours.

My point isn't that the president broke his wedding vows as many before and after have done and will do.
> Most of us break our vows in dozens of small ways at least:
> every time we do not honor our spouses, or love them fully,
> every time we criticize or demean, we break our vows.

I sympathize with the president's humanity. The point isn't even anymore whether he lied or that he lied.
> *The point is* that we are so willing to say to ourselves and to each other and to our children that it doesn't matter.
> > When we believe this doesn't matter, *we have been deceived*
> > > by the philosophy of this world that has degraded sex,
> > > that has devalued the meaning of commitment,
> > > that would have you think that fidelity and chastity are
> > > > hallmarks of an outdated morality for which we have
> > > > become too sophisticated.
> > *You did not so learn Christ!*

I was amused and sobered by an editorial inspired by the final episode of the situation comedy *Seinfeld* last year. This editor was an avid fan, but being a theologian, he also pointed up some problems with *Seinfeld*.

> Most disturbing in remembering "Seinfeld" is less the direct or indirect references to sex than the superficiality of human relationships that were dominated by the pursuit of casual, undemanding, and uncommitted sex. The "nothing" of the lives of these characters carried over into relationships with persons of the opposite sex. . . . [B]oth the pursuit of sex as the operative practical goal of life and

the insistence that it carry with it no commitment so dominated this show that it has to be seen as a major challenge to what Christian faith has claimed about both the locus of sexual activity in deeply committed human relationships and the divine intent that man and woman should find their life together in love and fidelity. Those two terms — love and fidelity — stand so forthrightly as code words for God's way with us and God's way for us, that the explicit rejection of both loving and faithful relationships in a program with such powerful influence on the popular consciousness has to be not only recognized but decried. . . . The moral issues raised by the presence and absence of "Seinfeld," therefore . . . confront us with a world where morality is shaped by the marketplace in the most direct way possible while reminding us that the biggest single player in the marketplace is television and its entertainment congeners whose moral yardstick, with few exceptions, is purely economical. It is unlikely that any large attack on the moral looseness of our contemporary life will achieve anything until it has found out how to deal with this 800-pound gorilla who joins us in our living room each evening. His only real interest is in finding enough bananas to consume.[8]

The author of Colossians would call that 800-pound gorilla the elemental spirits of the universe.

What we know so well is that we will not find our lives nestled in the bosom of that gorilla.

We will not find our life's meaning in gathering and collecting bananas for that gorilla.

We will not find quality, joy, harmony, peace, love, kindness,
    any of the qualities we find good and acceptable and perfect
      in life,
    we will not find these things joining in with any of those
      whose only focus is this world.

We will not find our lives or find our lives fundamentally better
    by pursuing the latest and the hottest and the fastest.

We will not find ourselves in *religious ritual.*

    There is not one right way to worship God.

---

8. Patrick D. Miller, "Good-bye Seinfeld," *Theology Today* 55 (July 1998): 149.

So do not submit to regulations:
>play only the pipe organ/play only the tambourine;
>raise your hands/don't raise your hands;
>say Amen/don't say Amen.
The high energy of the loudest gospel choir is not better or
>worse than the worship of monastic life.
>It is different. Worship God. Worship God in spirit and in
>>truth.

In Christ we have died to the arbitrary rules of this world.
We have died to arbitrary rules of religious life or religious
>ritual.
We have died to the primary value of needing the best, the
most, the fastest, the most titillating, the prettiest, the hottest, the
latest.
None of these things are bad in and of themselves.
>As a matter of fact they hold no particular value or debit.
Having the best, the most, the fastest, the hottest, the prettiest,
>is not necessarily a deficit in the Christian life.
It is, however, a tremendous weight and preoccupation that
>requires even more in terms of keeping one's primary focus
>>on God.
It's not that the things of the world are bad in and of themselves.
All these things were created by God, and those that were created by
us were done so because God gave us the godly gift of creativity.
But Paul talks about first things. Elemental things. Primary
>things.
>Therefore, do not look for your life in that which the world
>>would offer.
Set your minds on things that are above, not on things on
>earth.
>For you have died. And your life is hid with Christ in God.
You wonder where to go next? What to do? How to make that
>decision?
>How to create a life in an empty nest? How to create a life
>>alone?

Should you change jobs? Confront the boss? Confront the
      spouse?
Succumb to the temptations of what promises to be a disastrous
      relationship
    or to that which would be unfaithful or even adulterous?
What to do? How to know?

Your life can be found in one place.
    It can be found in nothing that is offered on this earth as of
      primary importance.
    It can be found only in Christ in God. That is of first order.

HELL'S HOPE

Romans 8:18-25
Isaiah 11:1-9

"Hell's Hope" was an advent sermon first prepared and preached for the First Presbyterian Church of Plainsboro, NJ, on December 1, 1996. Romans 8:18-25 was the primary text for the sermon. The Isaiah text played a part in the conversation, but was not as thoroughly exegeted as the Romans text. Following are some of my questions and observations regarding my initial conversations with the Romans text.

Most compelling during my early conversations with the text was the notion that the creation was subjected to futility and that the creation itself will be set free. I had always thought of this text as referring to the predicament of humanity, the fallen and lost condition in which we find ourselves as descendents of Adam and Eve. As I lived with the text for preaching, the fall of all creation, and the promise that the whole creation would one day be set free, took hold of my imagination. I carried many questions to my dialogue partners regarding the connection of the fallen creation to fallen humanity. "Groaning in travail" had always been such a human image for me, and obviously a feminine image. How did that groaning manifest itself in all humanity and in creation? What is the connection between eager longing and patience? Aren't the two conflictual?

My dialogue partners confirmed that when Adam and Eve fell, all of creation fell too, because humanity was given dominion and stewardship over creation. The resurrection life referred to in 8:21 is to be a part of complete creation. Reference is made here to Isaiah 11:6-9, and the peaceful pairings of animals which in our fallen state are natural enemies. The liberated life we live right now under the Lordship of Jesus Christ is within the circumstances of decay, φθορα. This decay is not merely synonymous with materiality. Believers are delivered within the circumstances of decay; those who live κατα σαρκα, according to the flesh, will suffer decay. When believers are delivered from decay, all creation will be delivered as well.

The connection of humanity to all creation, and the tension between patience and longing, drove this sermon. Furthermore, a pastoral concern was the kerygmatic expectation and affirmation that one day we will be delivered. The birthing image proved to be apt, tangible, and problematic at the same time. The idea is that humanity, along with creation, will be delivered after a season of interminable labor. The delivery promises to be fruitful in spite of the pain. The image is so strong it begs reflection in the sermon. The concern, however, is that some today still labor in vain. Despite our advanced technology in medical science, some women wait with eager longing, groan in travail, and yet delivery brings indescribable suffering when the child is stillborn, or is critically ill and dies, or is massively deformed. How does the preacher hold out this image of the promise of delivery when there may be those in the congregation for whom delivery meant profound grief and sadness?

In the end I used the image, trying to indicate that when human birthing brings not happy delivery but death, it is a manifestation of how we have not yet been delivered from the groaning and suffering of this age, what Paul calls the present, evil age. I further assuaged my pastoral concerns by thinking no one in the congregation had suffered such a loss recently, and I knew of no one in this particular congregation who had ever suffered such a loss, though I couldn't be sure. I found out two years after preaching the sermon that a new neighbor had come to church that day for the first time. And she was merely three months past such a loss. I was chastened by her report to me, from the safe distance of two years, of how she struggled in the context of that sermon to understand her loss. I'm still not certain if the sermon was helpful to her in the long run. The gospel and our words in sharing the gospel have tremendous power and must be handled with great care.

HELL'S HOPE

Isaiah 11:1-9
Romans 8:18-25

I often think when I listen to the evening news, that the newscasters should use the same disclaimer that is used of many TV movies and real-life, reenacted docudramas. "Based on a true story. Names, places, and dates have been changed." Based on the true story. The true story is the human story, and it is altogether too often the same old story.

Whether the refugees are Hutus from Zaire,

Muslims from Bosnia, Kurds from Iraq, Jews from Poland
. . . the story is always the same.

Age-old hatred, inhuman atrocities committed against fellow human beings.

It is *hellacious* what we are capable of doing to one another.

Whether the result of civil war, ethnic or racial or religious strife, we can never get used to it.

We can never get used to the hollow faces and the empty eyes and the bloated stomachs of terrified starving children — a veritable hell on earth.

The names, the places, the dates, they change, but the story always seems to be the same.

Hell takes on a different face, a different geographical location, but hell is hell.

We know it when we see it. We know it when we are confronted with it.

We know it when we are living it.

My earliest memory of starving children on the other side of the earth was of those in Biafra. As a child we were shamed into eating our veggies and wiping our plates clean because children were starving in Biafra. I never quite understood the connection, but I was moved nonetheless.

I still don't understand the connection between our empty plates and starving children around the world — after all, none of us is going to mail them our lima beans as we used to beg mother to do — but I have started to understand my mother's motivation.

It isn't that cleaning our plates will help those children.

It is making the connection between what we have and being grateful for what we have. It has to do with not whining or grumbling about having to eat healthy food when there are millions of children who die for want of it.

Sometimes the tragedy we witness at home and around the world is of our own making. On the other side of the world people die from starvation and disease because of warring factions.

Here at home people usually die a slower death, though not always.

> Babies who don't get their vaccinations,
> children who go to school malnourished,
> and children who wander from school to school
> > because their families are essentially homeless
> are but silent victims of our inability to take care of all of
> > our citizens.

We can't figure out how to get the job done.

> Should government make all of this happen?
> Should charitable donations?
> Should the churches and synagogues and mosques?
> Should the local communities?
> Shouldn't we be able to see to it that every child has a roof
> > over her head,
> > warm clothes to wear, and food in his belly when he
> > begins school?

We should be able to take care of these basic needs. We have the supplies. We have the technology. We can make it better! But we can't. We are human. The problems are intractable.

Even Jesus said we shall always have the poor with us. We no longer live in the garden of Eden. We bear the imprint of our fallen ancestors, Adam and Eve, and in this present evil age, we shall not escape the sufferings of this present time.

Sometimes the tragedy in our midst is of our own making. But other times we are simply at the mercy of the earth's whim. God charged Adam to take care of the earth, to be a steward of the earth. But when Adam fell from grace, the earth fell with him. We often don't do a very good job of taking care of the earth. And the earth often seems to be seeking its own revenge on us.

California, the land of my growing up, is a land of earthquake, fire, drought, and flood. My oldest brother is fond of saying California is a desert merely trying to reclaim itself.

We can water it, shore it up, cut fire trails, build aqueducts, plunge flexible concrete pilings ever farther into the surface of the planet, but the earth will have its own way with us and the result is often suffering, death, destruction, hell on earth.

For those who witness the destruction of land and people;
 for those in India for whom a flash flood only recently has
  meant the death of thousands;
 for the Rwandan or Hutu or Muslim refugee who has no home
  and for whom starvation and disease are a present reality,
 we must heed the cry of the one who mocked the Psalmist by
  saying, *"Where is your God?"*

Where is your God? On behalf of the eleven children left orphans by TWA Flight 800, we must hear the question, Where is your God?

From victim of flood and drought and terrorist we must hear the terrified cry, Where is your God?

From the cancer victim who leaves behind small children,
 from the hopelessly addicted substance abuser,
 from the well-meaning parents whose otherwise placid world is
  shattered when their small child is killed by a passenger-
  side air bag — for heaven's sake —
 we must hear the question, Where is your God?
For all of those who have lost hope, we must heed the cry,
 Where is your God?
 and from all those who have mocked us living in hope,
  we must hear with compassion, the cry, Where is your God?
From the scorched earth where hundreds of thousands of acres of

rainforest have been cleared, so immense an area, in fact, that astronauts report seeing the emptiness from space, from the scorched earth we can hear the cry, Where is your God?

From the thousands of miles of shoreline of coral reef that are destroyed by local village fishermen trying to scratch out a meager living, we can hear the groaning of the earth, Where is your God?

And the cry isn't new. Throughout the centuries the cry has gone up from creation and humanity, Where is your God?

What we experience today, and what humanity and all of creation has known throughout the millennia as hell on earth, is what the apostle Paul calls the sufferings of this present time.

Somehow we thought we could do better. With the Enlightenment, and the triumph of rational thinking, with the Industrial Revolution and the advance of modern technology, we thought we could do better.

In this modern age, we thought we could think our way out of all this suffering. Produce more food and distribute it more evenly. Build such massive weapons of destruction that no one would ever dare to really use one.

Forget massive weapons of destruction. We were in Washington, D.C., this weekend and you can no longer get anywhere near the White House in your car. Pennsylvania Avenue and all nearby accessible arteries are barricaded. It seems as though the White House is under siege. And in a sense it is. Who needs a high-tech nuclear device when a simple car bomb is enough to terrorize a city?

No, the modern age is coming to an end — in fact, the modern age is already at an end — and one telltale sign of the whimpering close of the modern era is that we have not been able to think our way out of the sufferings of this present time. Somehow our rationality and technology just aren't enough.

And so we are left, near the end of the second millennium in the
    common era,
    we are left with the cruel reality of hell on earth,
    and anyone who has ever lost a child,
    or come home to find a beloved spouse has died alone,
    or has lost a job with no backup means by which to support

a family,
or whose marriage has irreparably fallen apart,
or any who *want* to come home for Thanksgiving
but find themselves no longer welcome,
or anyone who empathizes with those persons whose images fill
our TV screens,
or with the beggar on the street . . . anyone of us . . .
there isn't a one of us, who doesn't know something about
hell on earth, the sufferings of this present time.

The apostle Paul captures the intensity of this groaning, the depth of the cry, the pain of the suffering, when he says the whole creation has been groaning as in the pains of childbirth right up to the present time, and not only the whole creation, but we ourselves.

All of humanity is groaning together in travail, as in the pains of childbirth, even we who have been saved by the gracious self-giving of our Lord Jesus, even we groan as we await the redemption of our bodies. Even we groan, because knowing Jesus doesn't mean we are strangers to hell.

But on this first Sunday of Advent,
amidst the sufferings of this present time, there is a hope
in hell.
The image of childbirth, of the creation groaning together in
travail, is the perfect image for suffering with hope for
delivery.

When I was pregnant with Anna, our first child, physically carrying this child was easy. But emotionally I was a wreck. I rode an emotional roller coaster that had incredible highs and lows. Along about the beginning of the ninth month, I began to wonder if there was really going to be a baby. I had heard the heartbeat. I felt her moving and kicking and hiccuping. But it seemed so long I began to wonder if this was a cruel hoax. There really wasn't a baby and I would feel this way for the rest of my life.

Of course, Anna came in due time. For many women and those

who go through childbirth with them, especially those who do it unanesthetized, you know the pain and suffering can be intense.

But it doesn't last forever.

In the end, most often, in the end there is new life,

the fulfillment of the promise of pregnancy,

the reward for the suffering endured in delivery.

And when, tragically, the promise of pregnancy is not fulfilled,

it is only further evidence of the suffering of this present

time.

Our hope is in the knowledge that our groaning is not empty. Our groaning and our suffering is not without purpose or perspective.

There is a hope in hell.

And the hope is in the promise of delivery,

the promise of the final redemption of our bodies,

the promise of a new life where there will be no suffering,

there will be no more tears.

God will wipe away our tears, death will be no more;

mourning and crying and pain will be no more.

As great as they are, the sufferings of this present time cannot even be compared to the glory that awaits us.

Small hope you say? Perhaps. Perhaps the hope of sharing in the glory of God is only a small tiny thread of a hope. But even the smallest shred of hope is what keeps us alive. It is what keeps us willing and wanting to do this life another day.

In those moments before dawn, before the promise of a new day is fulfilled — when in the breast of even the most devout Christian there occasionally beats the question, Where is your God? —

in the moment when the rainbow appears and the floodwater

subsides;

when the earth finally shudders its last aftershocks and lies

still;

when weary from fighting, men and women lay down their

arms at last in a moment of cosmic truce;

when we groan to know what hope a tomorrow might hold,

there comes a flicker of light.

167

In the darkness of the sufferings of the present age,
>there comes a flicker of light — a candle piercing the
>>predawn.
And by that flicker of light we are reminded once again that
>God came to us,
>>graciously, mercifully, humbly,
>>born of a young Jewish girl and her bewildered betrothed.
God's light came to us in that most poignant form of human
>hope,
>>a tiny little baby,
>>a newborn mewing for his milk and beginning his journey
>>>to the cross.
And the light, the light of hope as it points to the one by whom
>we are saved,
>>that light continues to shine in our darkness,
>>begging the answer to the question, Where is your God?

God is here. God is among us.
>God is in your heart and mind by the power of the Holy Spirit
>>who groans before God on our behalf.
By the power of the Holy Spirit, Jesus lives among us, empowering
>us, girding us up, encouraging us until that day for which we
>>await with eager longing
>as a woman heavy with child groans in labor.
We wait for that day because we know no other day will do,
>but no other day is needed.

We wait for that day, and in our longing and our groaning,
>*we pray.*
>We don't have the words to pray.
>>We don't have lofty words of wisdom,
>>>of which Paul didn't think too highly anyway.
>We do not even know what to pray for.
>We don't even know what is the will of God.
>Certainly healing, wholeness, reconciliation. Jesus prayed for as
much with his disciples just before he left them.

But in this present evil age, in this hell on earth, what does that look like? Perhaps it looks like divorce — Jesus seemed to understand that sometimes in this life, divorce is the answer. That's why he said divorce must be fair and just.

Perhaps it will look like merciful death. Paul seemed to understand this. That's why he said to live is Christ and to die is gain.

We don't know exactly what to pray for, but we pray and we wait, and we groan, together with the whole creation.

And while we wait we celebrate with joy the gift of the Christ child whose birth and death and resurrection mean life to us.

But we also wait with eager longing for that day when Christ shall come again.

We wait for that day when the fullness of God's salvation will be revealed. Not only we ourselves, but the earth which is our home waits with eager longing for the coming of Christ again when the age-old hatreds will cease,

when the glory of God's love will obliterate any earthly power that does not bow down and humble itself before the Almighty.

> We long for the day when natural enemies shall be at peace,
> when predator is no longer enemy to its prey.
> We wait for that day when the wolf shall lie down with the
> lamb,
> the leopard shall lie down with the kid,
> the calf and the lion and the fatling together,
> and a little child shall lead them.
> They will not hurt or destroy on all God's holy mountain,
> for the earth shall be full of the knowledge of the Lord,
> as the water covers the sea.
> And in that day the glory of the Lord shall be revealed.
> And the earth and all flesh shall see it together.
> For the mouth of the Lord has spoken.

169

APPENDIX

Hermeneutical Journey Report

A Hermeneutical Journey Report (HJR) is a summary of the journey of interpretation a preacher has traveled from the time the preaching text is chosen, to the final preparation of the sermon. I ask for a report on the whole journey based on the premise that the critical exegesis of a biblical text is only one part of the interpretation process that begins with the choice of a text (or topic) and culminates in the preaching of the sermon.

The goal of the hermeneutical journey is the sermon. The critical exegetical work that is done with the text is guided by the questions, concerns, and congregational needs that the preacher brings to the text. The HJR has ingredients similar to a more traditional exegesis report, except that the goal is the final sermon, not an exegetical paper. The exegetical details included in the report will be those that demonstrate the preacher's conversation with dialogue partners in response to the preacher's questions, and those that most influenced the shaping of the sermon.

The most important first step in dealing with a text for preaching, and therefore, in the HJR, is the dialogue between the preacher and the text. What questions does the preacher have of the text? What concerns does the text raise? What are the questions and challenges the text presents to the preacher? Reporting on this dialogue, often with a single-spaced list of questions, is most essential. What are the preacher's guesses as to the meaning of the text?

170

Next, the HJR should reflect the conversation the preacher had with dialogue partners. How did one's dialogue partners, such as biblical linguists, commentators, and theologians, answer the preacher's questions? What new questions were raised? The HJR should reflect the swing back and forth from one-on-one conversation with the biblical text, to conversation with dialogue partners, and back again to the text.

Paul Scott Wilson provides a helpful model for the early listening in "An Initial Literary Reading of a Biblical Text," in *The Practice of Preaching*, pp. 133ff. The exegetical method suggested by Thomas G. Long in *The Witness of Preaching*, pp. 48-77, is a helpful model for the conversation with dialogue partners, with added emphasis on the relationship of the preacher and the text.

The report should conclude with at least a paragraph indicating how the preacher moved from this work with the text and dialogue partners to the sermon. What is the compelling direction of the sermon? What moved the swing around the circle? The instructor should have a general sense at the end of the HJR what the sermon is going to be about, and be able to see clearly how the preacher got there.

Bibliography

Achtemeier, Paul J. "Finding the Way to Paul's Theology: A Response to J. Christiaan Beker." In *Pauline Theology, Vol. 1: Thessalonians, Philippians, Galatians, Philemon,* edited by Jouette M. Bassler. Minneapolis: Fortress Press, 1991.

Allen, Ronald J. *Preaching the Topical Sermon.* Louisville: Westminster/John Knox Press, 1992.

Bailey, Raymond. *Hermeneutics for Preaching: Approaches to Contemporary Interpretations of Scripture.* Nashville: Broadman Press, 1992.

Banks, Robert J. *Paul's Idea of Community.* Peabody, MA: Hendrickson Publishers, 1994.

Barrett, C. K. *Paul: An Introduction to His Thought.* Louisville: Westminster/John Knox Press, 1994.

Barth, Karl. *Church Dogmatics.* Edited by Bromiley and Torrance. Edinburgh: T. & T. Clark, 1956.

———. *The Word of God and the Word of Man.* Translated by Douglas Horton. Gloucester, MA: Peter Smith, 1978.

Bartow, Charles L. *God's Human Speech: A Practical Theology of Proclamation.* Grand Rapids: Eerdmans, 1997.

Beker, Johan Christiaan. *Paul the Apostle: The Triumph of God in Life and Thought.* Philadelphia: Fortress Press, 1980.

———. "Recasting Pauline Theology: The Coherence-Contingency

Scheme as Interpretive Model." In *Pauline Theology, Vol. 1: Thessalonians, Philippians, Galatians, Philemon,* edited by Jouette M. Bassler. Minneapolis: Fortress Press, 1991.

———. *The Triumph of God: The Essence of Paul's Thought.* Translated by Loren T. Stuckenbruck. Minneapolis: Fortress Press, 1990.

Browning, Don S. *A Fundamental Practical Theology.* Minneapolis: Fortress Press, 1996.

———. *Religious Thought and the Modern Psychologies: A Critical Conversation in the Theology of Culture.* Philadelphia: Fortress Press, 1987.

Bruce, F. F. *The Epistles to the Colossians, to Philemon, and to the Ephesians.* The New International Commentary on the New Testament. Grand Rapids: Eerdmans, 1984.

Buttrick, David. *Homiletic: Moves and Structures.* Philadelphia: Fortress Press, 1987.

Buttrick, George Arthur, ed. *The Interpreter's Bible.* Nashville: Abingdon Press, 1984.

Calvin, John. *Institutes of the Christian Religion.* Edited by John T. McNeill. Philadelphia: The Westminster Press, 1960.

Candlish, Robert S. "The Pious Dead are Lost — Living Believers are Miserable." In *Great Sermons on the Resurrection of Christ, by Celebrated Preachers with Biographical Sketches and Bibliographies.* Compiled by Wilbur M. Smith. Natick, MA: W. A. Wilde Co., 1964.

Chadwick, Henry, ed. *The Acts of the Apostles.* Harper's New Testament Commentaries. New York: Harper & Row, 1957.

Charry, Ellen. *By the Renewing of Your Minds: The Pastoral Function of Christian Doctrine.* New York: Oxford University Press, 1997.

Cousar, Charles B. *The Letters of Paul.* Nashville: Abingdon Press, 1996.

Craddock, Fred B. *Overhearing the Gospel.* Nashville: Abingdon Press, 1978.

Ebeling, Gerhard. *Word and Faith.* Philadelphia: Fortress Press, 1963.

Eslinger, Richard L. *A New Hearing: Living Options in Homiletic Method.* Nashville: Abingdon Press, 1987.

Fant, Clyde E., Jr., and William M. Pinson, Jr., eds. *Twenty Centuries of Great Preaching, Volume Two: Luther to Massillon.* Waco, TX: Word Books, 1971.

Farley, Edward. "Preaching the Bible and Gospel." *Theology Today* 51 (April 1994): 90-103.

Felder, Cain Hope, ed. *Stony the Road We Trod: African American Biblical Interpretation.* Minneapolis: Fortress Press, 1991.

Frei, Hans. *The Identity of Jesus Christ: The Hermeneutical Bases of Dogmatic Theology.* Philadelphia: Fortress Press, 1975.

Gillespie, Thomas W. "Friend of Mine." *Princeton Theological Seminary Bulletin,* n.s., 20 (1999): 243-46.

————. *The First Theologians: A Study in Early Christian Prophecy.* Grand Rapids: Eerdmans, 1994.

Greenhaw, David M. "The Formation of Consciousness." In *Preaching as a Theological Task,* edited by Thomas G. Long and Edward Farley, 1-16. Louisville: Westminster/John Knox Press, 1996.

Gross, Nancy Lammers. "A Re-Examination of Recent Homiletical Theories in Light of the Hermeneutical Theory of Paul Ricoeur," an unpublished doctoral dissertation submitted to the Faculty of Princeton Theological Seminary, 1992.

Gutierrez, Gustavo. *A Theology of Liberation.* Maryknoll, NY: Orbis Books, 1973.

Haenchen, Ernst. *The Acts of the Apostles.* Philadelphia: Westminster Press, 1971.

Hirsch, E. D., Jr. *Validity in Interpretation.* New Haven: Yale University Press, 1967.

Jewett, Paul. *Paul: The Apostle to America.* Louisville: Westminster/John Knox Press, 1994.

Kay, James F. "The Word of the Cross at the Turn of the Ages." *Interpretation* 53 (January 1999): 44-56.

Keener, Craig. *The IVP Bible Background Commentary: New Testament.* Downers Grove, IL: InterVarsity Press, 1993.

Killinger, John. *Fundamentals of Preaching.* Philadelphia: Fortress Press, 1985.

Kim, Eunjoo Mary. *Preaching the Presence of God: A Homiletic from an Asian American Perspective.* Valley Forge, PA: Judson Press, 1999.

Klemm, David E. *The Hermeneutical Theory of Paul Ricoeur.* London: Associated University Presses, Inc., 1983.

Kraus, C. Norman. *The Community of the Spirit: How the Church is in the World.* Scottdale, PA: Herald Press, 1993.

Long, Thomas G. Review of *Homiletic,* by David Buttrick. *Theology Today* 45 (April 1988): 108, 110-12.

————. *Preaching and the Literary Forms of the Bible.* Philadelphia: Fortress Press, 1989.

————. *The Witness of Preaching.* Louisville: Westminster/John Knox Press, 1989.

Martin, Ralph P., Daniel G. Reid, and Gerald F. Hawthorne, eds., *A Dictionary of Paul and His Letters: A Compendium of Contemporary Biblical Scholarship.* Downers Grove, IL: InterVarsity Press, 1993.

Martyn, J. Louis. *Theological Issues in the Letters of Paul.* Nashville: Abingdon Press, 1997.

McGrath, Alister E. *Christian Theology: An Introduction.* Oxford: Blackwell, 1994.

McKim, Donald K., ed. *A Guide to Contemporary Hermeneutics: Major Trends in Biblical Interpretation.* Grand Rapids: Eerdmans, 1986.

Migliore, Daniel L. *Faith Seeking Understanding.* Grand Rapids: Eerdmans, 1991.

Miller, Donald G. *The Way to Biblical Preaching.* Asheville: Abingdon Press, 1957.

Miller, Patrick D. "Good-bye Seinfeld." *Theology Today* 55 (July 1998): 149.

Munck, Johannes. *The Acts of the Apostles.* The Anchor Bible 31. New York: Doubleday, 1967.

Musser, Donald W., and Joseph L. Price, eds. *A New Handbook of Christian Theology.* Nashville: Abingdon Press, 1992.

Packer, J. W. *Acts of the Apostles.* Cambridge: Cambridge University Press, 1966.

Palmer, Richard E. *Hermeneutics: Interpretation Theory in Schleier-*

macher, Dilthey, Heidegger, and Gadamer. Evanston: Northwestern University Press, 1969.

Patte, Daniel. *Preaching Paul.* Philadelphia: Fortress Press, 1984.

Polanyi, Michael. *The Tacit Dimension.* Gloucester, MA: Peter Smith, 1983.

Read, David H. C. "The Perils of Preaching." *Princeton Seminary Bulletin,* n.s. 6, no. 3 (1985): 168-78.

Ricoeur, Paul. *Essays on Biblical Interpretation.* Edited by Lewis S. Mudge. Philadelphia: Fortress Press, 1980.

————. *Interpretation Theory: Discourse and the Surplus of Meaning.* Fort Worth, TX: Texas Christian University Press, 1976.

Schleiermacher, Friedrich. *Brief Outline on the Study of Theology.* Translated by Terrence N. Tice. Richmond, VA: John Knox Press, 1966.

Smith, Christine M., ed. *Preaching Justice: Ethnic and Cultural Perspectives.* Cleveland: United Church Press, 1998.

Sweazey, George E. *Preaching the Good News.* Englewood Cliffs, NJ: Prentice-Hall, 1976.

Thiselton, Anthony C. *The Two Horizons: New Testament Hermeneutics and Philosophical Description with Special Reference to Heidegger, Bultmann, Gadamer, and Wittgenstein.* Grand Rapids: Eerdmans, 1980.

Thompson, James W. *Preaching Like Paul: Homiletical Wisdom for Today.* Louisville: Westminster/John Knox Press, 2001.

Tracy, David. "The Foundations of Practical Theology." In *Practical Theology: The Emerging Field in Theology, Church, and World,* 61-82. Edited by Don S. Browning. San Francisco: Harper & Row, 1983.

van Leeuwen, Theodoor Marius. *Surplus of Meaning: Ontology and Eschatology in the Philosophy of Paul Ricoeur.* Amsterdam: Rodopi, 1981.

Westberg, Granger E. "The Christian and Grief." In *Rockefeller Chapel Sermons of Recent Years.* Compiled by Donovan E. Smucker. Chicago: The University of Chicago Press, 1967.

Wilson, Paul Scott. *The Practice of Preaching.* Nashville: Abingdon Press, 1995.

Wink, Walter. *Naming the Powers: The Language of Power in the New Testament*. Philadelphia: Fortress Press, 1984.

Wright, N. T. *What Saint Paul Really Said: Was Paul of Tarsus the Real Founder of Christianity?* Grand Rapids: Eerdmans, 1997.

Subject Index

179

Scripture Index